A Kalmus Classic Edition

Johann Sebastian
BACH

NOTEBOOK FOR ANNA MAGDALENA BACH

FOR PIANO

K 02131

CONTENTS

Partita in A Minor
    Prelude..8
    Allemande...13
    Courante..15
    Sarabande..18
    Menuet..20
    Gigue..22

Partita in E Minor
    Prelude..26
    Allemande...36
    Courante..39
    Sarabande..45
    Tempo di Gavotta................................49
    Gigue..50

Menuet in F Major..56
Menuet in G Major...57
Menuet in G Minor...58
Rondeau in B Major (Couperin).....................59
Menuet in G Major...62
Polonaise in F Major......................................63
Menuet in B Major...65
Polonaise in G Minor.....................................66
Chorale "Wer nur den lieben Gott lasst walten"...67
Chorale in F Major...68
Chorale "Gib dich zufrieden"........................69
Menuet in A Minor..71
Menuet in C Minor..72
March in D Major..73
Polonaise in G Minor.....................................74
March in G Major..76
Polonaise in G Minor.....................................77
Aria "So oft ich meine Tobacks-Pfeife"........78

Menuet in G Major (Bohm)..........................82
Musette in D Major..83
March in E-flat Major....................................84
Polonaise in D Minor....................................86
Aria "Bist du bei mir"....................................87
Sarabande in G Major....................................89
Solo per il Cembalo in B Major....................91
Polonaise in G Major.....................................94
Prelude in C Major...96

Suite No. 1 in D Minor
    Allemande...99
    Courante..101
    Sarabande..103
    Menuet I...104
    Menuet II..105
    Gigue..107

Suite No. 2 in C Minor
    Allemande...110
    Courante..113
    Sarabande..115

Untitled Piece in F Major.............................117
Aria "Warum betrübst du dich"..................118
Recitative and Aria "Schlummert ein ihr matten Augen"....119
Chorale "Schaff's mit mir, Gott"..................128
Menuet in D Minor.......................................129
Aria "Willst du dein Herz mir schenken"...130
Chorale "Dir, dir Jehovah, will ich singen"
    Four voices..132
    Solo voice..134
Aria "Wie wohl ist mir, o Freund der Seelen".....136
Aria "Gedenke doch, mein Geist, zurücke"......138
Chorale "O Ewigkeit, du Donnerwort".......140

PREFACE

The copying of music nowadays is done for professional reasons only, by the student of composition or the professional copyist. There was a time, however, when it belonged to the habitual occupations of the music lover in general. While in early 18th century Germany there was no actual dearth of printed matter, copies still were rare, due to the lack of a well-organized system of distribution. Besides, to possess merely a printed copy was not truly owning the composition in the more personal sense of the word. Music was too much regarded as a living thing to be confined exclusively to the realm of goods that could be bought in the store. Even if the listening or performing experience preceded or followed the act of purchase, the true music lover was not satisfied: the piece had to be copied in order to become really and intimately his own.

In Bach's family several of these "Notenbüchlein" were in circulation. We know three of them: the "Klavierbüchlein" for J.S. Bach's eldest son Friedemann (started 1720 in Köthen), a second one without any title from 1722, containing the first five French Suites and some smaller pieces, and finally the one from 1725, which bears the name of J.S. Bach's second wife for good reasons. It is the one we present in this reprint, which follows the Callwey edition of 1935. The preface and the notes are by Arnold Schering and still represent the latest results of musicological research, which had entered only spottily into the first complete edition of Dr. Richard Batka of 1906.

The original copy (Preussische Staatsbibliothek, Berlin) must have been a true delight for the eye when it was new. It was covered with green paper over a hard base, with pressed-in gold rims, two locks and a red silk ribbon. On the cover we find three large gilded letters:

AMB
1725

which later were supplemented by Philipp Emanuel to "Anna Magdal. Bach." Without any doubt a master of the book binding craft in Leipzig had been ordered to do an especially careful and beautiful job on it. And it must have been Johann Sebastian who gave the order, possibly with the intention to give the book to his wife in 1725 as a birthday present.

Anna Magdalena, born on September 22, 1701, was the daughter of the court and field trumpeter Johann Caspar Wuelcken, who was employed in Zeitz at the time of her birth. Bach, who was widowed since 1720, made her acquaintance in Köthen, where she was engaged as "Fürstliche Sängerin." It must have been music that brought them together, for Bach was the conductor of the court music of the prince in Köthen. They were married there on December 3, 1721. Two years later the couple moved to Leipzig, where the "court singer" changed to a very bourgeois "Frau Kantor" and a loving and conscientious mother, who gave birth to thirteen children between 1723 and 1742. She survived Bach by ten years, dying in pitiful circumstances on February 27, 1760, as an "Almosenfrau" (woman dependent on charity). From the little we know about her it is safe to assume that she was an amiable woman and devoted wife, very serious in her domestic and family duties, participating at the same time in her husband's work to the best of her abilities. According to Johann Sebastian, she sang a decent soprano ("einen sauberen Sopran") in the house concerts of the family. Many compositions of Johann Sebastian have been preserved in her clear and faultless handwriting, and more than a third of the pieces in the Notenbüchlein have been copied by her.

There have been some misconceptions (caused partly by Philipp Spitta) about the part which Johann Sebastian played in respect to the "Notenbüchlein." He had no influence on its final shape. After he had started it out by copying two of his piano-suites for it, he left it to its fate. After that, he seems to have been aware of its existence only occasionally. It can neither be proved that the book was meant to contain exclusively his own compositions nor that he intended to improve Anna Magdalena's piano playing. Without any doubt it was left to Anna Magdalena to decide what the book should contain. She accepted what she liked, and that was not only refined and profound music of her husband, but the easier, gallant art of smaller masters as well. It took a number of years, probably more than five, to fill the book. In the meantime, the children grew up. They asked for pretty pieces in the gallant style, for menuets, marches, polonaises, which they could play themselves and, not less important, execute after the rules of the art of dance. To keep the education of the children up to socially acceptable standards, one had to engage a "Tanzmeister," a master of dance, to teach them not only dancing, but graceful social manners, "die zierliche conduite," as well. It was necessary to collect simple, suitable pieces for such purposes, with a melody which could easily be taken by the fiddle of the dance master or by a flute. To do this was within Anna Magdalena's realm of duties, as Johann Sebastian had more important things to attend to. This explains the appearance of all the small, gracious "Spielstücke" (play-pieces) in the book. We can be sure that Bach, as a composer, had no part in them. They don't testify in any respect to Anna Magdalena's personal taste which, to judge from her upbringing and career, had been formed by music of a different style.

Besides, the children themselves occasionally tried a composition or the realization of a choral. Mother's "Notenbüchlein," dear to every one of them, served handsomely for this purpose. When Johann Sebastian happened to catch them unexpectedly in these endeavors, he corrected hastily the mistakes of the eleven-year-old Philipp Emanuel or dictated a few of the fundamental rules about intervals and figuring. It would not make any sense to assume that the latter were meant for Anna Magdalena's use. The simple, if not outright poor formulation of these rules at the end of the book is perfectly well-adapted for the intellectual capacity of children. Besides, they are incomplete and seem to have been written down hastily. The end of No. 7 has been omitted; this shows that the writer was not able to follow his father's dictation, which might have been fast, perhaps accompanied by demonstrations at the clavichord.

Furthermore, in Johann Sebastian's musical family life there were many occasions for the performance of special compositions, like weddings, christenings, birthdays, deaths, and social gatherings of all kind. No matter who was the author of these pieces, a stranger or a member of the family, the suitable place to put them down was Mother's musical family book. The second half of the book is filled with them, beginning with the song of the tobacco pipe on page 78. All these pieces have the quality of "Gelegenheitsstücke," of being composed for special occasions the nature of which can of course only be a matter of speculation. In any case, during the course of years, all kinds of compositions, serious and fun, important and unimportant, piled up on these sheets. No matter what the book originally was meant to be, the result was a hodgepodge of everything. It is this quality in particular which makes the book so attractive.

Johann Sebastian contributed only little to it. We can distinguish his hand clearly from the one of Anna Magdalena, who was a perfect artist in calligraphic music-copying. Several other handwritings can be recognized. There is a childish, unskilled one which seems to have been Philipp Emanuel's; and another one, more orderly, probably Wilhelm Friedemann's, who was a little older. The notation of the song "Willst du dein Herz mir schenken" shows a completely strange hand; it must have been written by someone who was not a member of the Bach family.

Our edition keeps as closely to the original as possible. Wherever it was necessary, the compositions have been provided with a new thorough bass-realization. No printed edition, of course, can truly substitute for the handwritten original in which accident and planlessness played such an important part. Many peculiarities and oddities of its contents can be revealed only by the facsimile edition. Modern print and bookmaking prevent the inclusion of the characteristic features of the personal handwritings, the various degrees of carefulness, the significant traces of usage and wear and the undefinable spiritual element in this precious relic. Only the factual, material contents can be given and here, too, we have to face limits. In view of many mistakes in writing, errors, omissions, corrections in all pieces which did not originate from Johann Sebastian's hand a strictly philological reproduction is impossible. A correct list of all errors would fill a volume in itself; but that would do too much honor to the careless writers. The critical edition of the book which the Bach-Gesellschaft published in 1894 did not contain a list of all mistakes, and we can do without it all the more as our edition is meant for practical use.

P. 8-25. This is the third of the six "Partitas" which Bach collected in 1731 as the first part of the "Klavierübung." They had been published separately since 1726. In Bach's own handwriting. This version is not quite identical with the printed (later) one. The printed edition includes a "Scherzo" before the end and calls the Prelude "Fantasia," the Menuet "Burlesca."

P. 26-55. The sixth of the "Partitas" (see above). In Bach's own handwriting. Here, too, deviations from the printed version are noticeable (especially in the Sarabande p. 45); none of them, however, being essential. For obvious reasons the Prelude is called "Toccata" in print. The "Notenbüchlein" does not include the "Air" and gives the Gigue alla breve, with dotted eighths, while the later edition chooses full measures with dotted quarter-notes.

P. 56-58. Three Minuets. Author unknown. (Handwriting of Anna Magdalena.)

P. 59. Rondeau. This composition is by Francois Couperin and can be found in the second volume of his "Pieces de Clavecin" (about 1715) with the heading "Les Moissonneurs" (The Harvesters).

P. 62-66. Two groups of one minuet and one polonaise each. Author unknown. Handwriting of Anna Magdalena.

P. 67. Chorale: "Wer nur den lieben Gott lässt walten." Added to the title is a handwritten remark by Philipp Emanuel: "By J.S. Bach." This composition is included in Kirnberger's collection of Bach's chorales for the organ (see vol. 40, p. 4 in the edition of the Bach-Gesellschaft). It might have been sung in Bach's house on festive occasions, to the accompaniment of the house-organ.

P. 68. This unfigured movement is based on the melody to Paul Gerhardt's church hymn "Gib dich zufrieden und sei stille." It does not give the text, however. In the "Notenbüchlein," only the outer voices (soprano and bass) have been written out except for the fermata bars, where the full five-voiced chord is given. The author of the melody is unknown. It can be found in Balthasar Koenig's "Gesangbuch" of 1738, slightly different in notation and with different basses. For Schemelli's "Gesangbuch" Bach wrote figured basses to another musical version (by J. Hintze, 1670) of the same text, which seems to have attracted him deeply. (See the next two paragraphs.)

P. 69. "Gib dich zufrieden und sei stille." A handwritten remark by Philipp Emanuel, to be considered as a most reliable source, points to J.S. Bach as the author of this composition, which has been written down both times by Johann Sebastian himself. The first arrangement is in G minor and in an unusually high range, which must be explained by the low pitch of the clavichord in Bach's time. The second, slightly different arrangement in E minor was apparently meant for the harpsichord or the house-organ. The text has been written out by Bach for the G minor arrangement, but our edition gives the words with the E minor version to make vocal execution to the accompaniment of modern instruments possible.

P. 71-77. Two minuets, marches, and polonaises by unknown authors. The possibility of Bach having any part in the conception of these simple period pieces in the "gallant" style has to be ruled out completely. Instrumentalists with some skill in reading thorough bass will have no difficulty in filling out the emptiness of the two-part arrangements by adding parts in both hands.

P. 78-79. Aria: "So oft ich meine Tabakspfeife." The poem has the title: "Erbauliche Gedanken eines Tabakrauchers" (elevating thoughts of a tobacco smoker). It is a rather delicious mixture of philistine humor and religious seriousness. The composition has been written down twice in succession, first by an unknown hand, without text and starting with D, the second time (by Anna Magdalena) with the text of the first stanza, but one fourth higher (starting with G) in order to make accompaniment on the clavichord possible. The composition presumably originated within the Sperontes-circle in Leipzig. (Sperontes was the editor of the "Singende Muse an der Pleisse," a collection of odes and songs of a partly spiritual, partly "down-to-earth" quality.) Bach as author is out of the question. The complete text has been put down much later (about 1780) on a separate sheet by a strange hand, the original copy having presumably been lost.

P. 82. Minuet. Probably by Georg Böhm, the organist and former teacher of Bach in Luneburg (d. 1733). This is indicated by the intimate "Mons." (monsieur) before the name. In Bach's handwriting.

P. 83. This graceful Musette (with so-called Murky-Basses) is close to the operatic style of the Hamburg composer Reinhard Keiser (1739). Handwriting of Anna Magdalena.

P. 84. March of unknown origin. Handwriting of Anna Magdalena.

P. 86. This untitled piece is a polonaise. The author is unknown; handwriting of Anna Magdalena.

P. 87. "Bist du bei mir." Known exclusively through the "Notenbüchlein." This melody seems comparatively high for voices (like "Gib dich zufrieden," p. 69) on account of the low clavichord pitch.

P. 89. Untitled piano piece in the character of a Sarabande. It is identical with the Aria-Theme of the Goldberg-Variations from the fourth part of the "Klavierübung" (about 1742; ed. of the Bach-Gesellschaft Vol. 3, p. 263). It seems doubtful that Bach was the composer; the modulations as well as the ornaments point to a style different from his.

P. 91. "Solo per il cembalo." Not by Bach. Handwriting of Anna Magdalena.

P. 94. Polonaise of unknown origin. Handwriting of Anna Magdalena.

P. 96. The C Major prelude from the first part of the "Well-Tempered Clavichord." Handwriting of Anna Magdalena. The first half of the composition has been put down on the left side of the book. The continuation, which originally was on the following right page, has been cut out together with some other pages. Anna Magdalena continued the copy on a new page, but omitted five bars, which we have supplemented in this edition.

P. 99-109. The first of the so-called French Suites (D minor). We find it already, in Bach's own handwriting, in the smaller "Notenbüchlein" from 1722. It dates back to the Köthen period. Handwriting of Anna Magdalena; minor deviations in regard to notation and ornaments.

P. 110-116. The first movements of the second French Suites (C minor), which also, in Bach's handwriting, can be found in the smaller "Notenbüchlein" of 1722. The copy of our book was written by Anna Magdalena. The end of the Sarabande and the three last movements (Air, Minuet, Gigue) are missing.

P. 117. Rather clumsy attempt of a single composition, corrected by a strange hand.

P. 118. Aria: "Warum betrübst du dich." The author of the text is unknown. The original melody hardly could have been Bach's; he added to it, however, and provided it with his own basses, thus conveying something of his spirit and touch to the composition. (In a similar way he treated the melodies of the Gesangbuch of Schemelli.)

P. 119-127. Recitative "Ich habe genug" and Aria: "Schlummert ein, ihr matten Augen." Both pieces are known as parts of the Cantata "Ich habe genug" (probably 1731 or 1732; edition of the Bach-Gesellschaft vol. 20, 36). There they are a major third lower (the Aria in E-flat Major) and have to be sung by a bass-voice. Besides, however, Bach left a soprano version of this Cantata (incomplete; edition of Bach-Gesellschaft, vol. 20, preface p.

XIV). The copy in our "Notenbüchlein" (handwriting of Anna Magdalena) seems to be the earliest version. The bass-aria of the Cantata is accompanied by string-quartet, while our soprano-aria requires only the accompaniment of the clavichord or harpsichord. The "Notenbüchlein" shows just the melody with the bare unfigured bass. Our realization of the bass is adapted to the style of the keyboard instrument; the complicated string quartet arrangement, which Bach uses in the Cantata, would have been out of place.

This aria has been written down twice: the first time only the vocal part, without taking care of the bass-system (p. 120), the second time with the bass part, but without the ending. Both copies are separated from each other. In both instances the writer must have been called away from her work, without having found the time to finish it. Six pages have been cut between p. 129 and p. 130, which points to some further disturbance at the time of these writings. Both versions have no instrumental prelude and vary, besides, in regard to the length of the interludes. Our edition supplements everything missing except for the prelude, according to the cantata version.

P. 128. Chorale: "Schaff's mit mir, gott." The text by Benjamin Schmolck was new at the time, having been published without melody in the "Dresdener Gesangbuch" (1723). The composer of the melody is unknown. Bach did only the figuring of the bass. Handwriting of Anna Magdalena.

P. 130. Aria di Giovannini: "Willst du dein Herz mir schenken." The origin of this famous love song is still a matter of dispute; all signs indicate, however, that Bach was not the author. He was in the habit of indicating his authorship clearly and unmistakably. We also have to reject the hypothesis that Giovannini stands for the pet name "Hänschen," hinting in a jocular way at Bach's first name. It would belittle the profound respect which Bach enjoyed in public and in his family.

The name refers without any doubt to the Italian composer Giovannini, who lived in Germany for a number of years and seems to have had perfect command of the German language. His seven German songs published in the third and fourth part of the collection of odes by Joahann Friedrich Gräfe (1741, 1743) show the same quality of elegant daintiness that characterizes our Love Song in the "Notenbüchlein"; Giovannini was an adherent of "Anakreontik" in music. In both places we find the little ornaments in the vocal part, which point to the mannerisms of the Italian Canzonetta style. "Willst du dein Herz mir schenken," however, surpasses Giovannini's other songs in charm and nicety of structure. This is not the only instance of a second-rate talent succeeding in creating a seemingly immortal masterpiece.

About the origin of the text nothing is known. Philipp Spitta, however, pointed to older jocular poems with similar contents. (Vierteljahrsschrift für Musikwissenschaft I, 1885, p. 62 ff. and 350 ff.). — Text and music are in different handwritings, both unknown to us. The writing of the text shows lack of experience. The pages are loosely added to the book. The first page originally did not belong to it at all, and altogether the relationship of the copy to its environment remains problematical. (See the "Revisionsbericht" in vol. 43 of the Bach-Gesellschaft edition, p. XIII f.)

P. 132. "Dir, dir, Jehovah, will ich singen." In four parts, by Johann Sebastian Bach. The poem is by Barthol Crasselius (1724). Bach's own handwriting.

P. 134. The same composition, with only the outer voices written out, perhaps to gain space for the complete text of all the (8) stanzas. Bach included this version of the magnificent piece in his arrangements for the "Gesangbuch" of Schemelli.

P. 136. "Wie wohl ist mir, o Freund der Seelen." The poem is by Wolfgang Chr. Dessler (d. 1722). We do not know the author of the melody; Bach is out of the question. He would not have permitted the "Nacht des Traurens" (night of sorrow) to be sung to the same notes as the "Angenehmen Freuden" (pleasant joys); furthermore, he would not have repeated four bars without any variation in the refrain. The composition is of particular beauty nevertheless. Busoni paid homage to it in his second violin sonata. Handwriting of Anna Magdalena.

P. 138. Aria: "Gedenke doch, mein Geist." The author of the text is unknown. It seems justified to attribute this beautiful spiritual slumber song to Johann Sebastian Bach.

P. 140. Chorale: "O Ewigkeit, du Donnerwort." The text is by Joh. Rist, the melody by Joh. Schop (1644). We used Philipp Emanuel Bach's arrangement of the middle voices in his edition of his father's four-part chorales (III. part, 1786, no. 274), the melody and bass parts being the same in both cases. Handwriting of Anna Magdalena.

PARTITA
in A Minor

JOHANN SEBASTIAN BACH

Prèlude

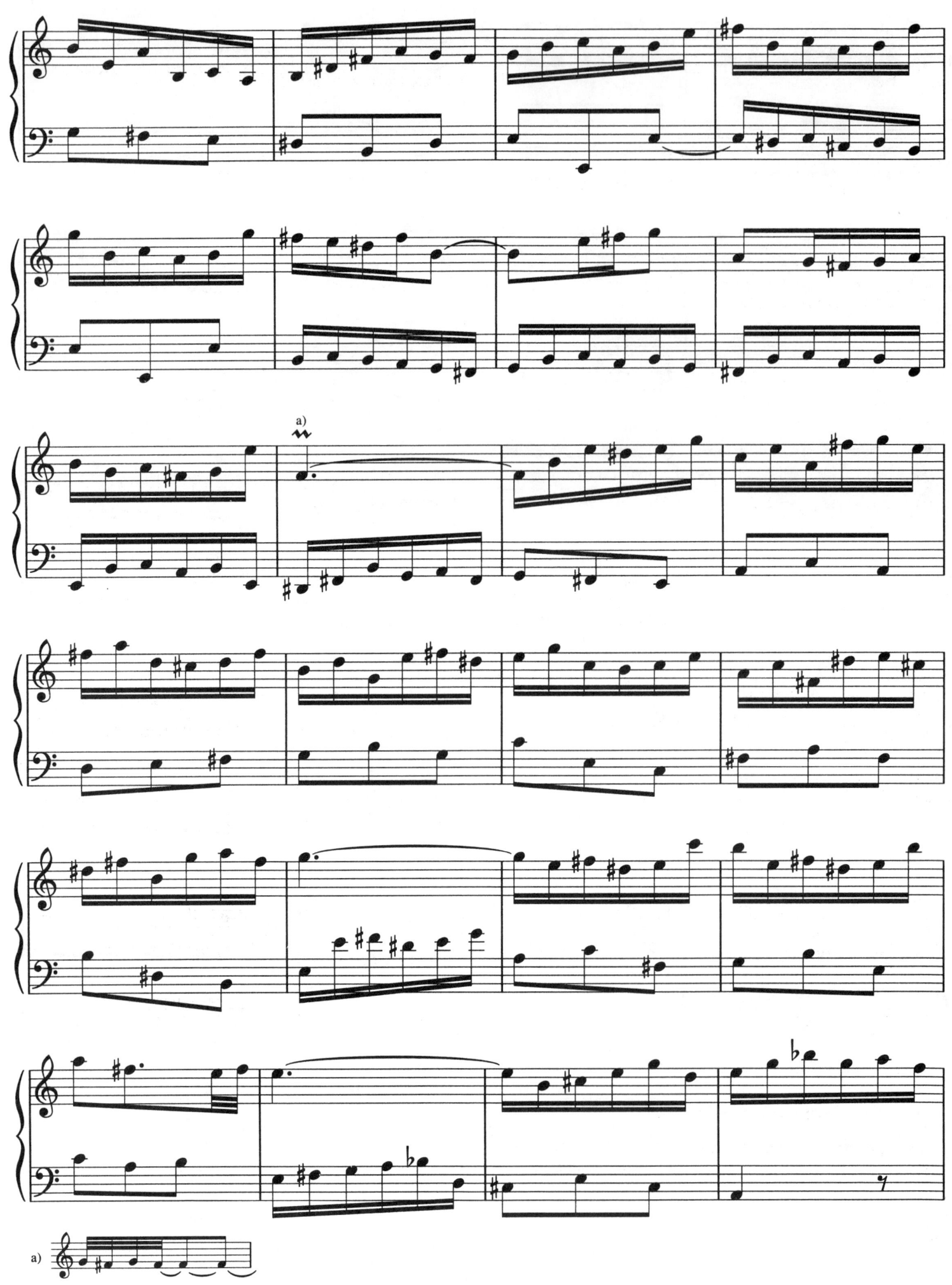

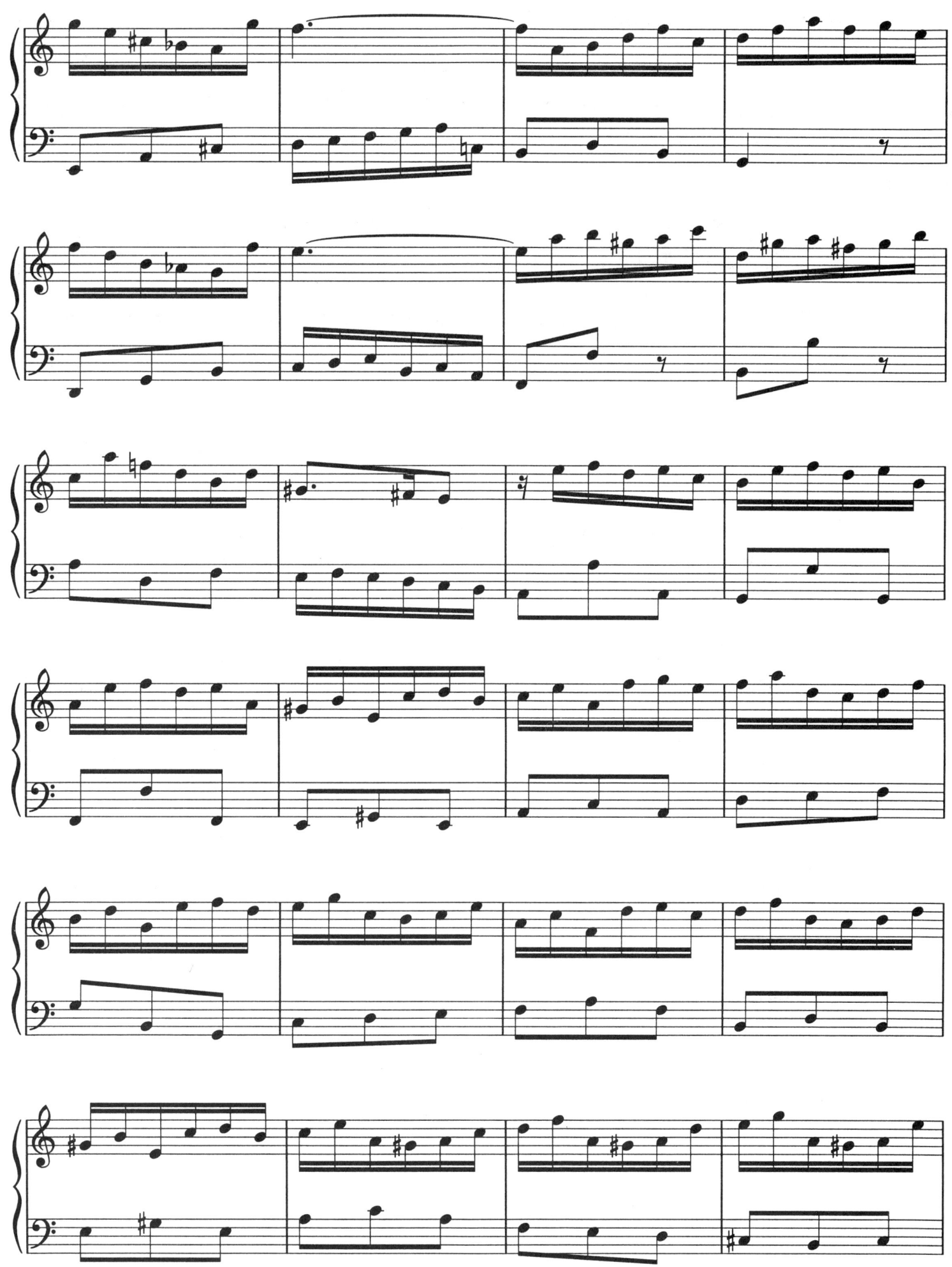

Allemande

16

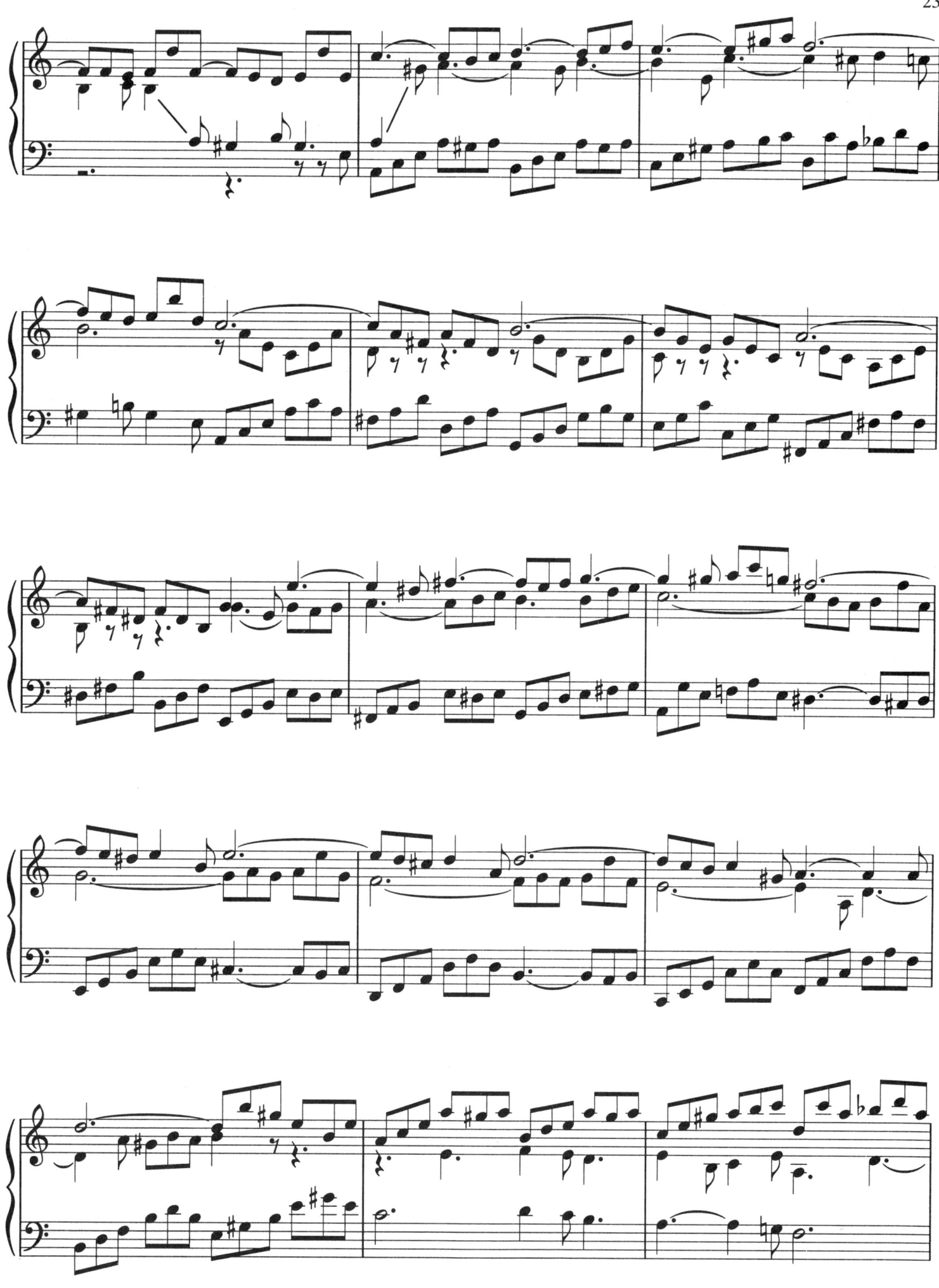

PARTITA
in E Minor

JOHANN SEBASTIAN BACH

27

34

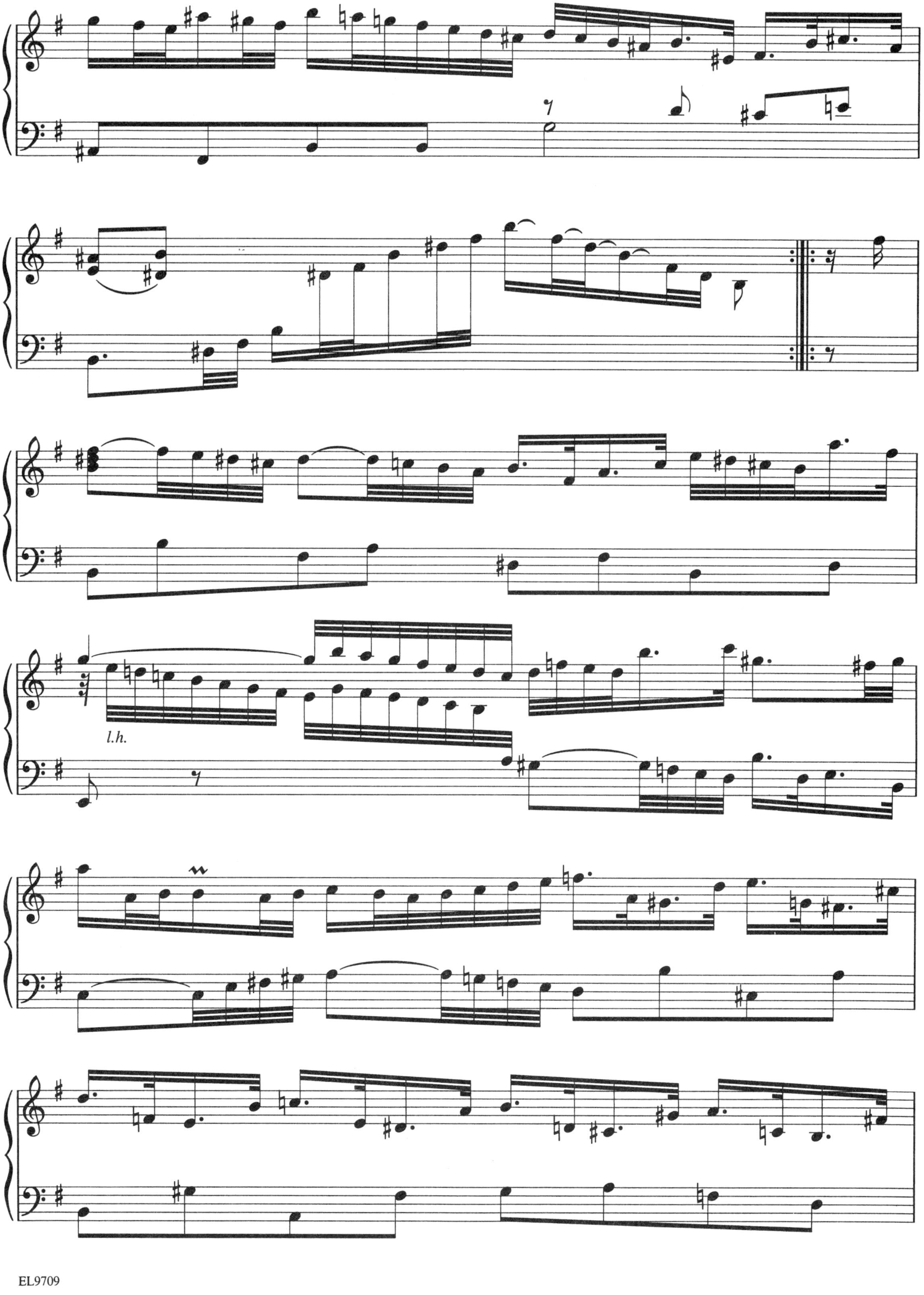
l.h.

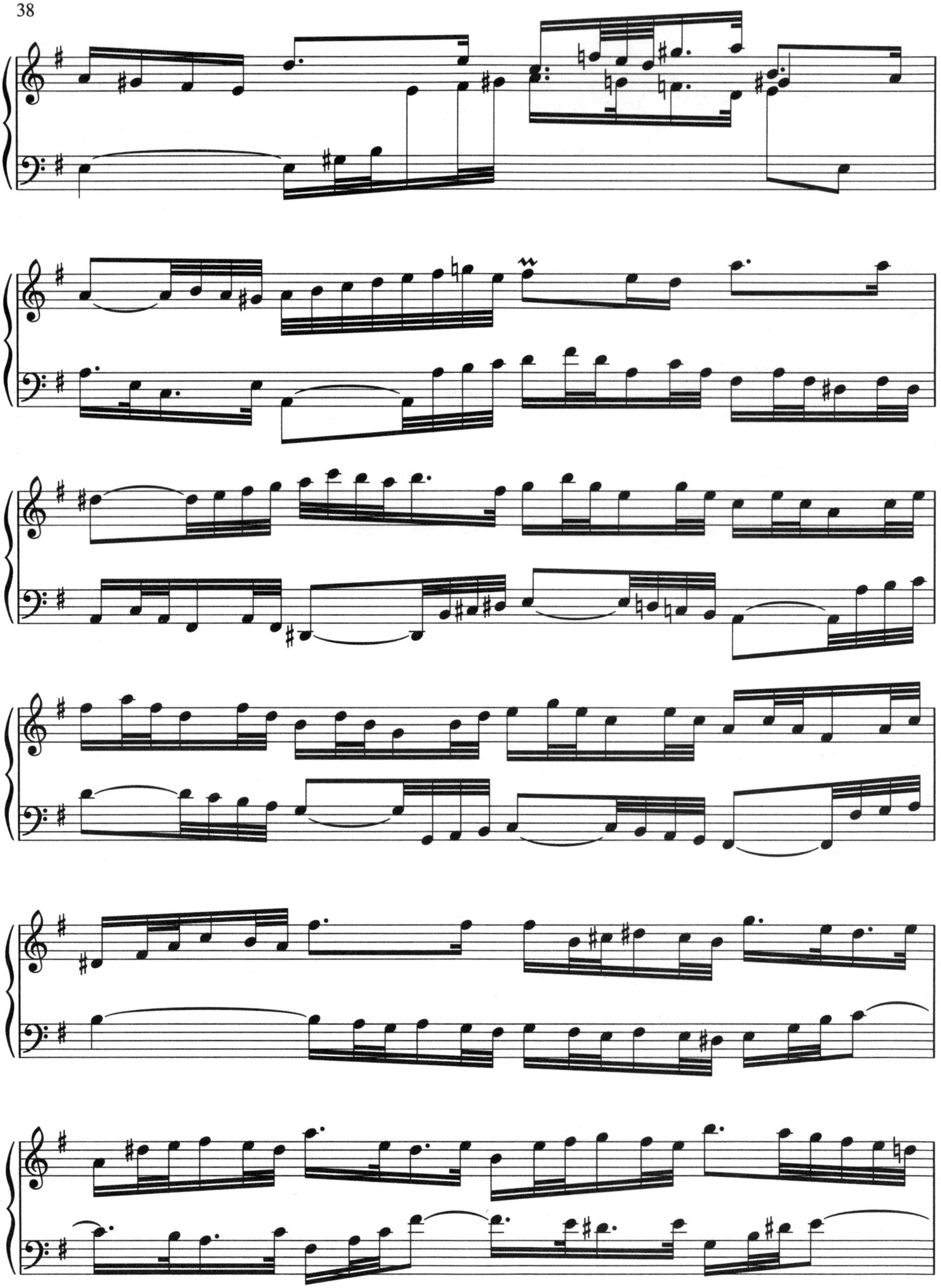

Courante

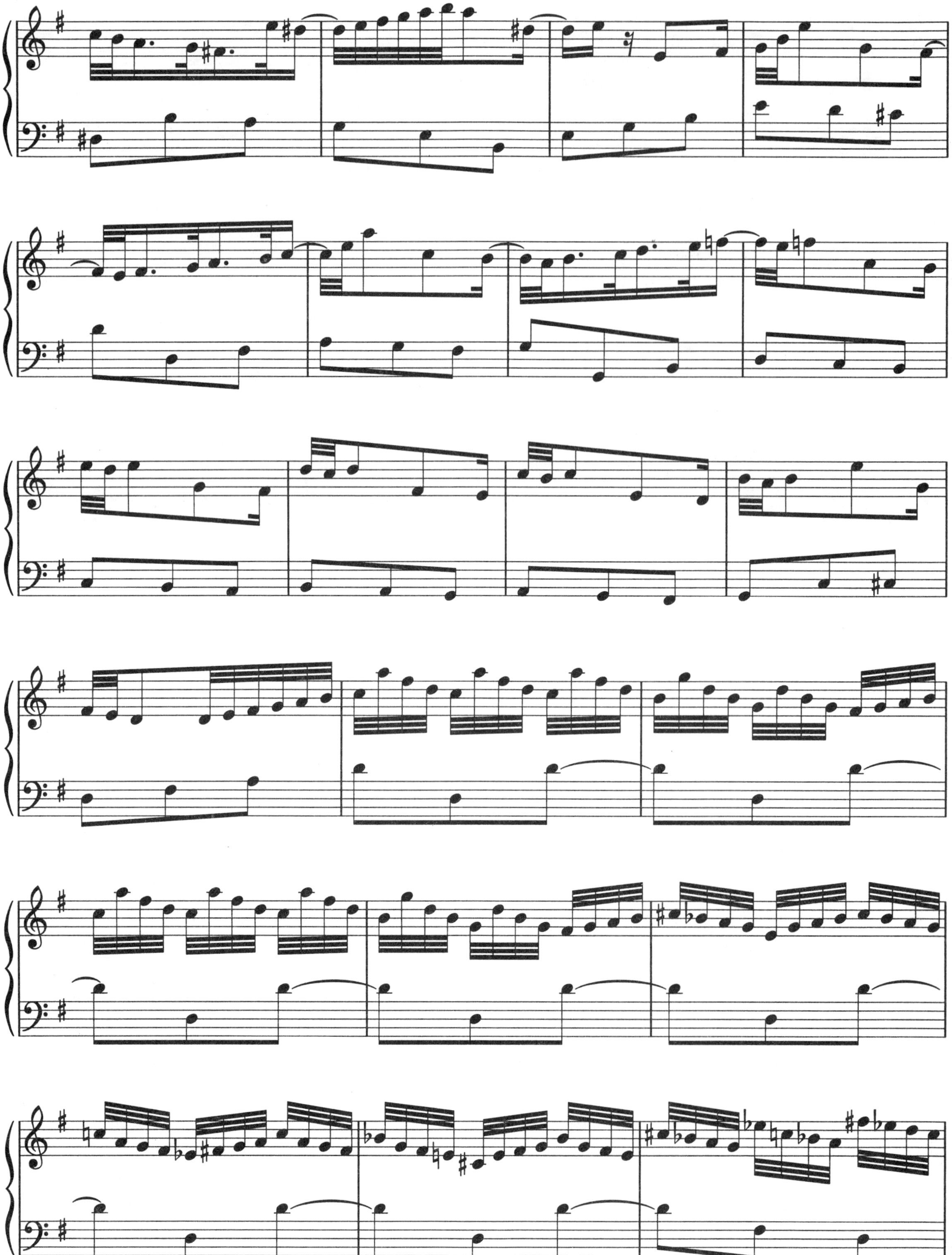

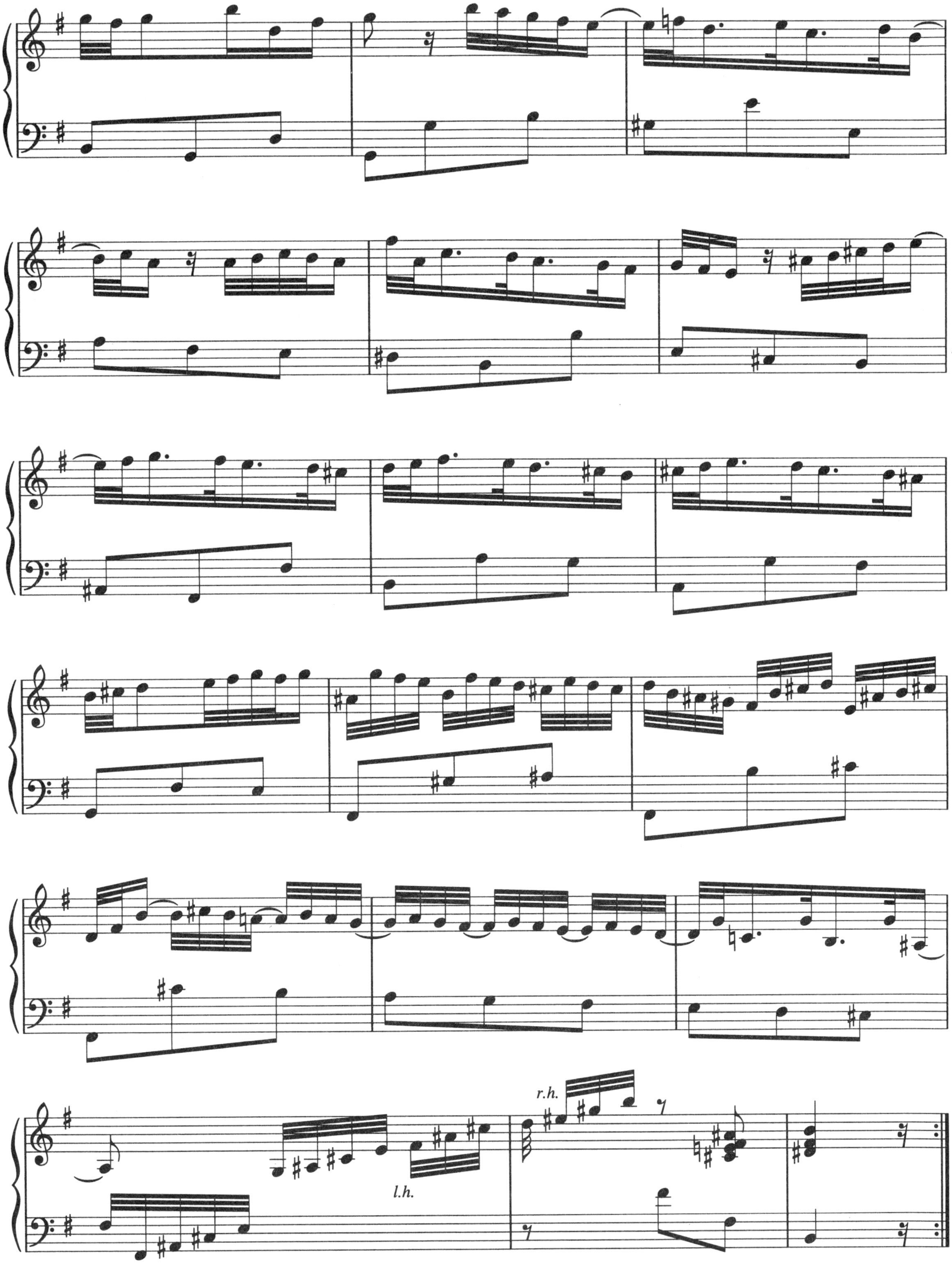
r.h.
l.h.

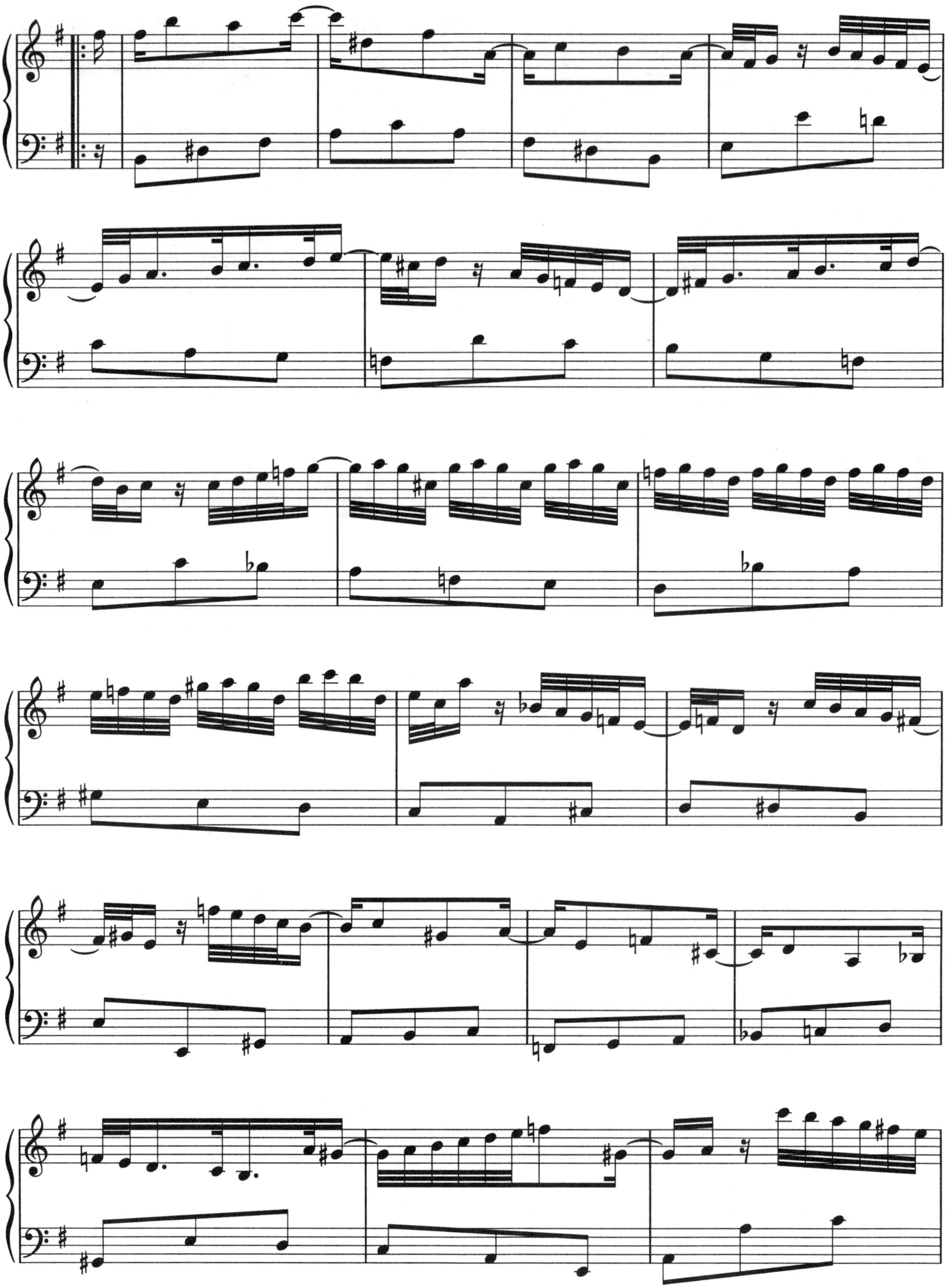

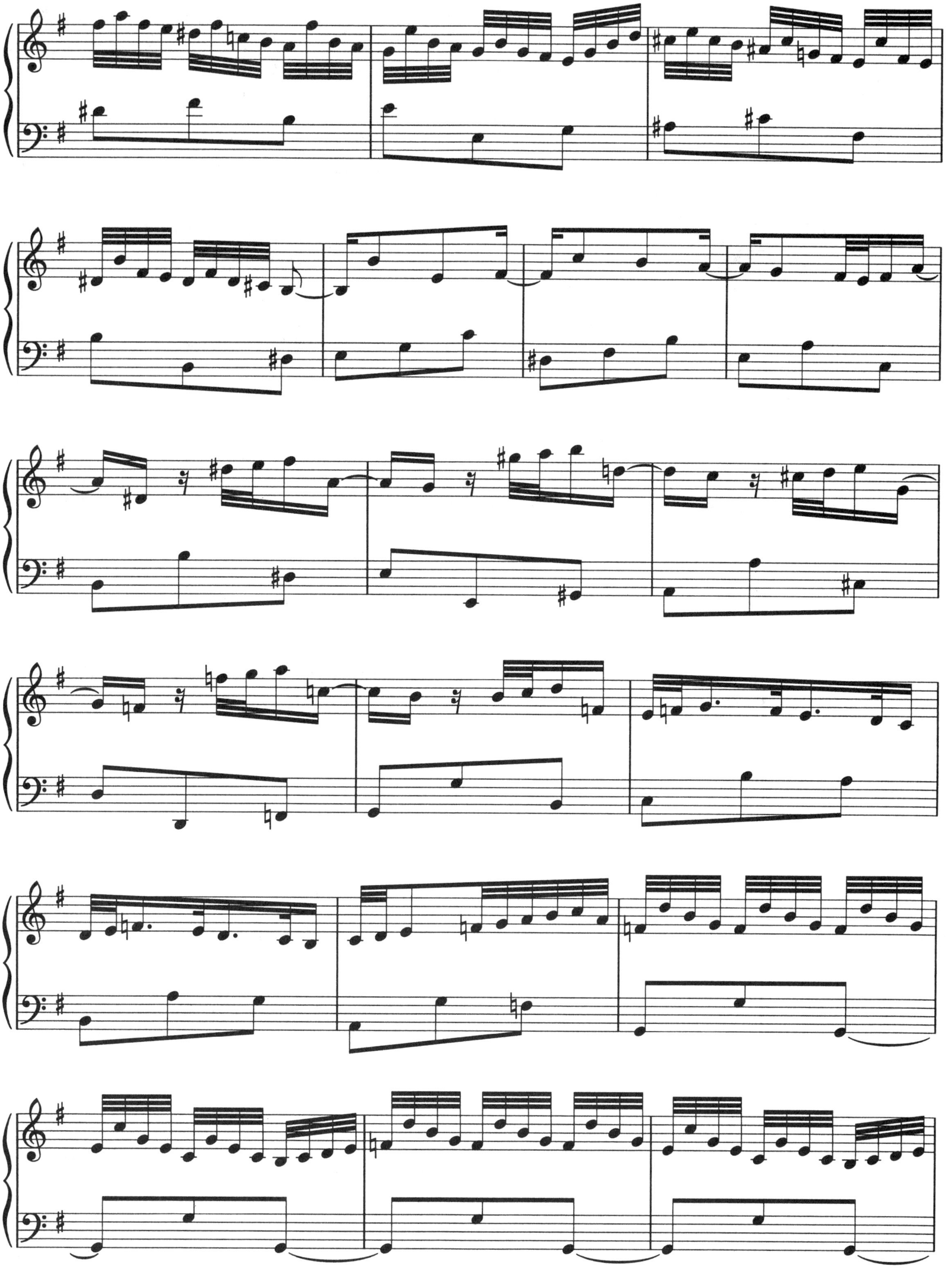

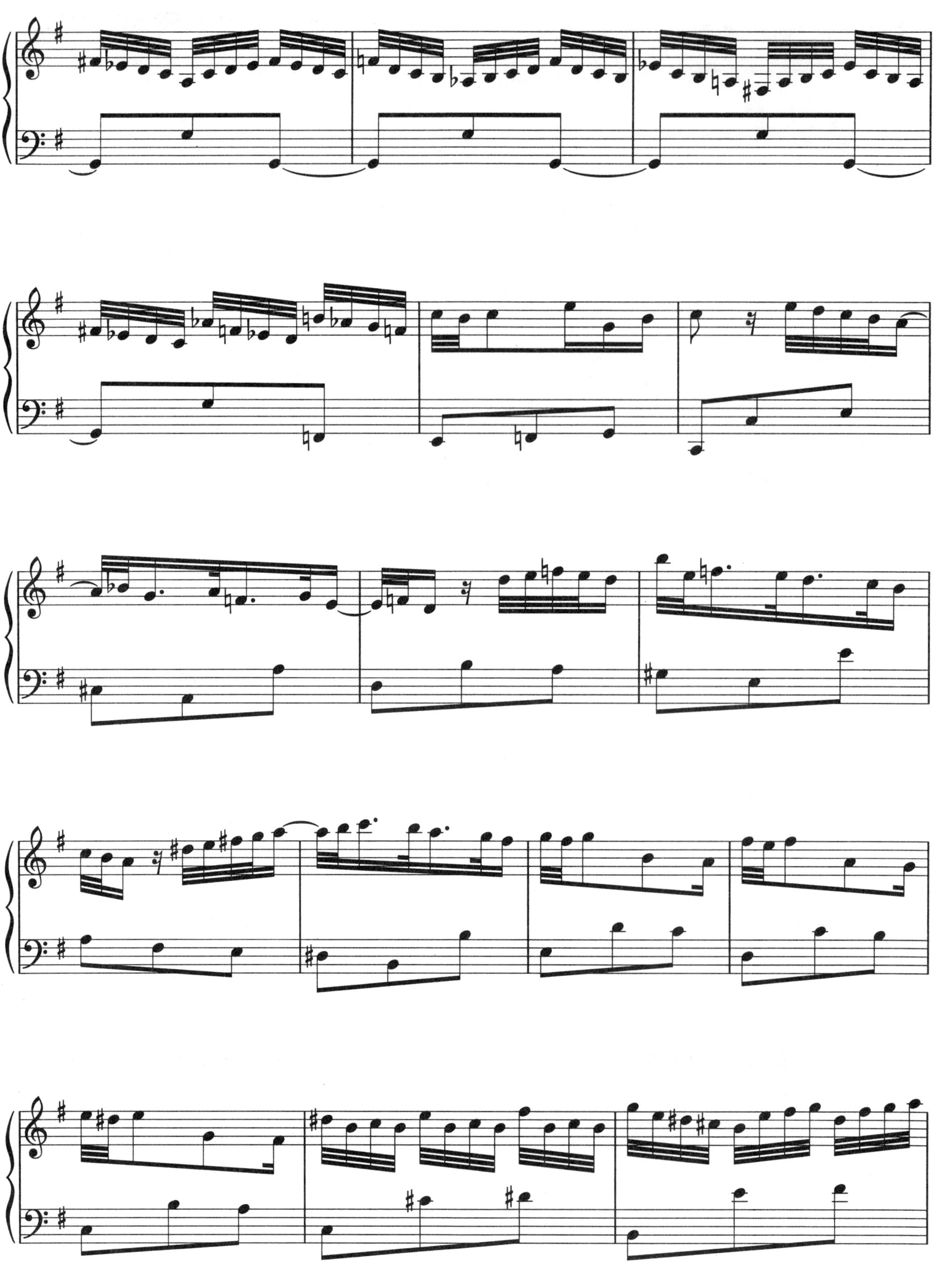

Sarabande

* Play as a rolled chord.   b)

46

47

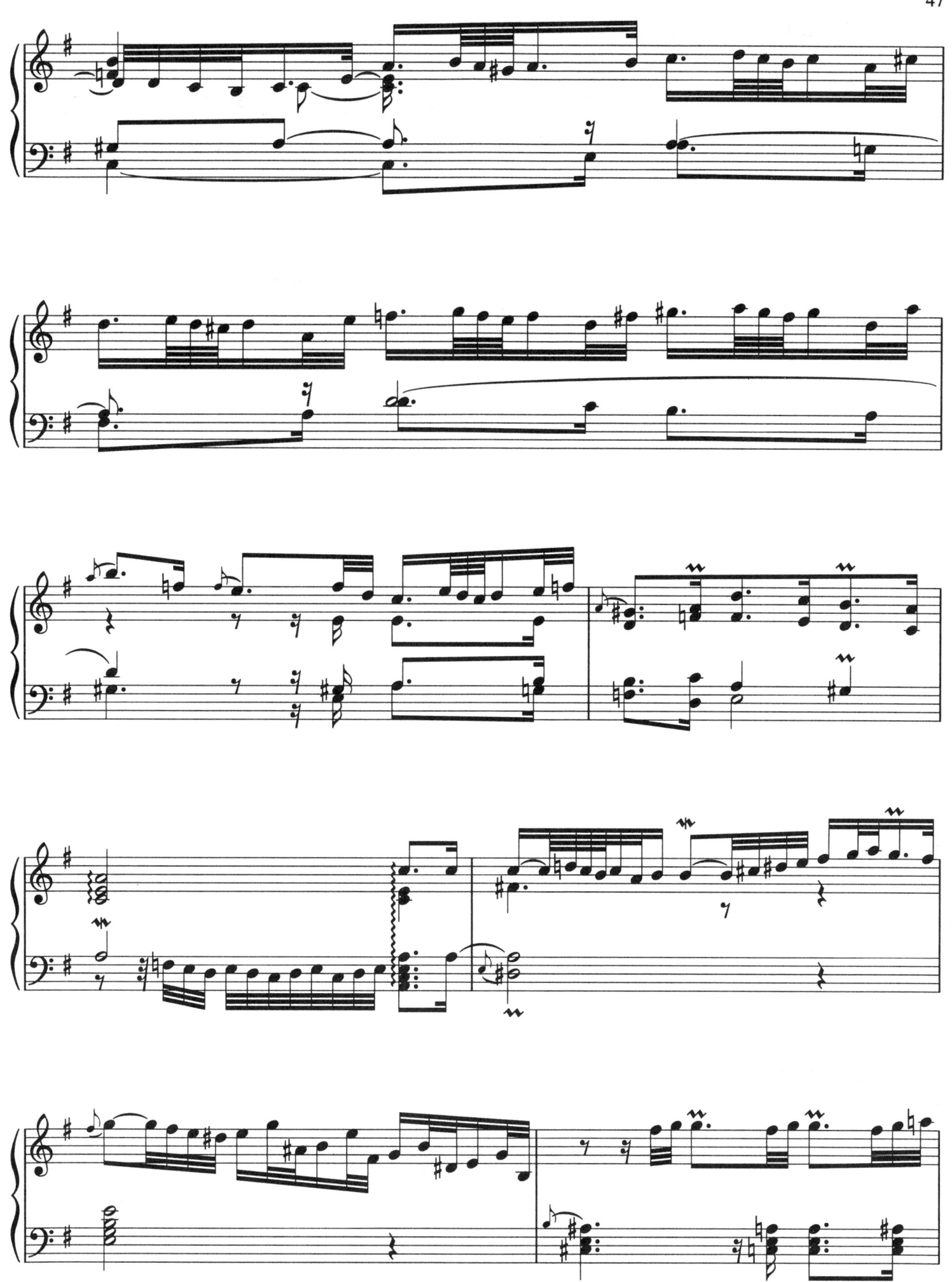

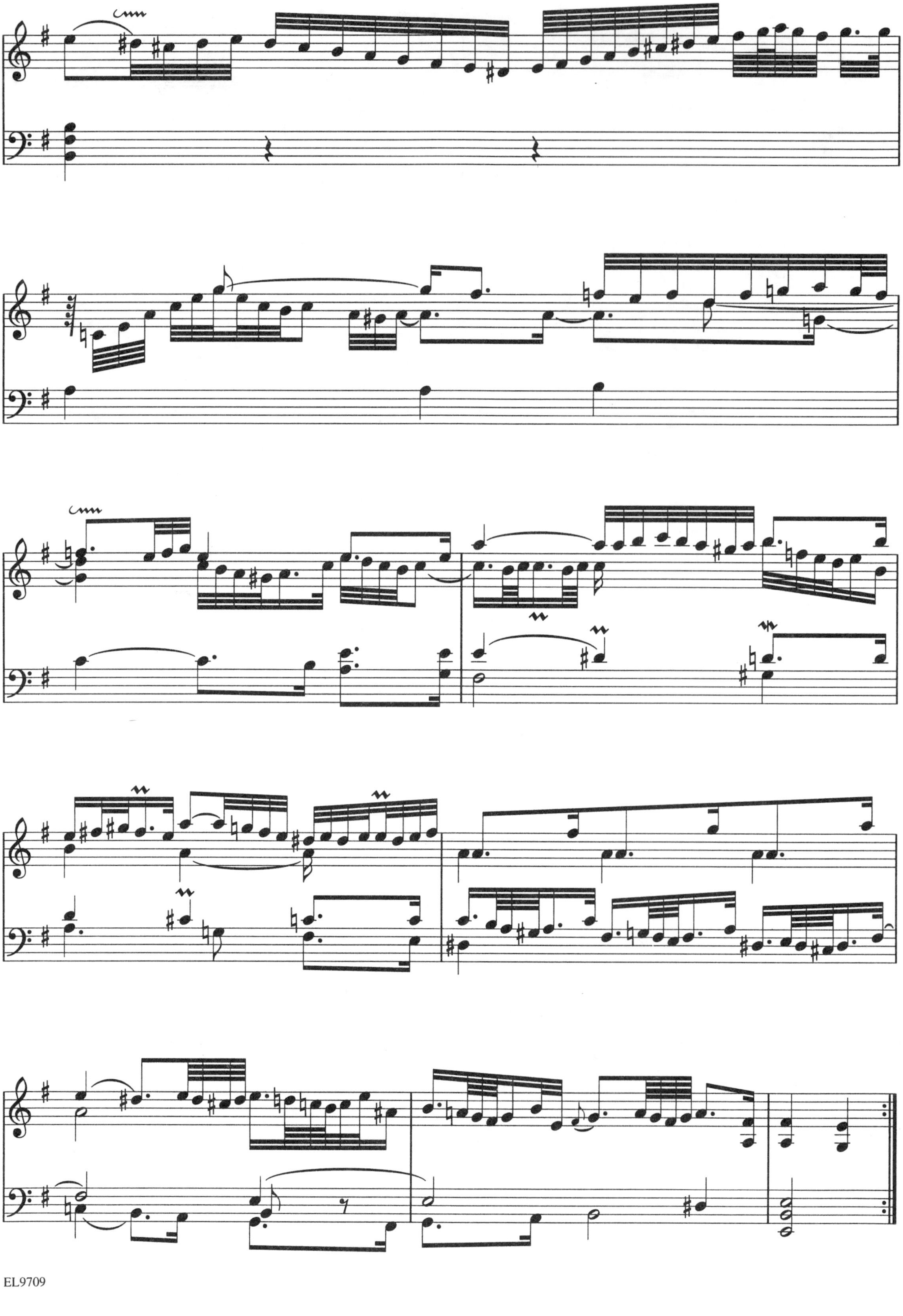

Tempo di Gavotta

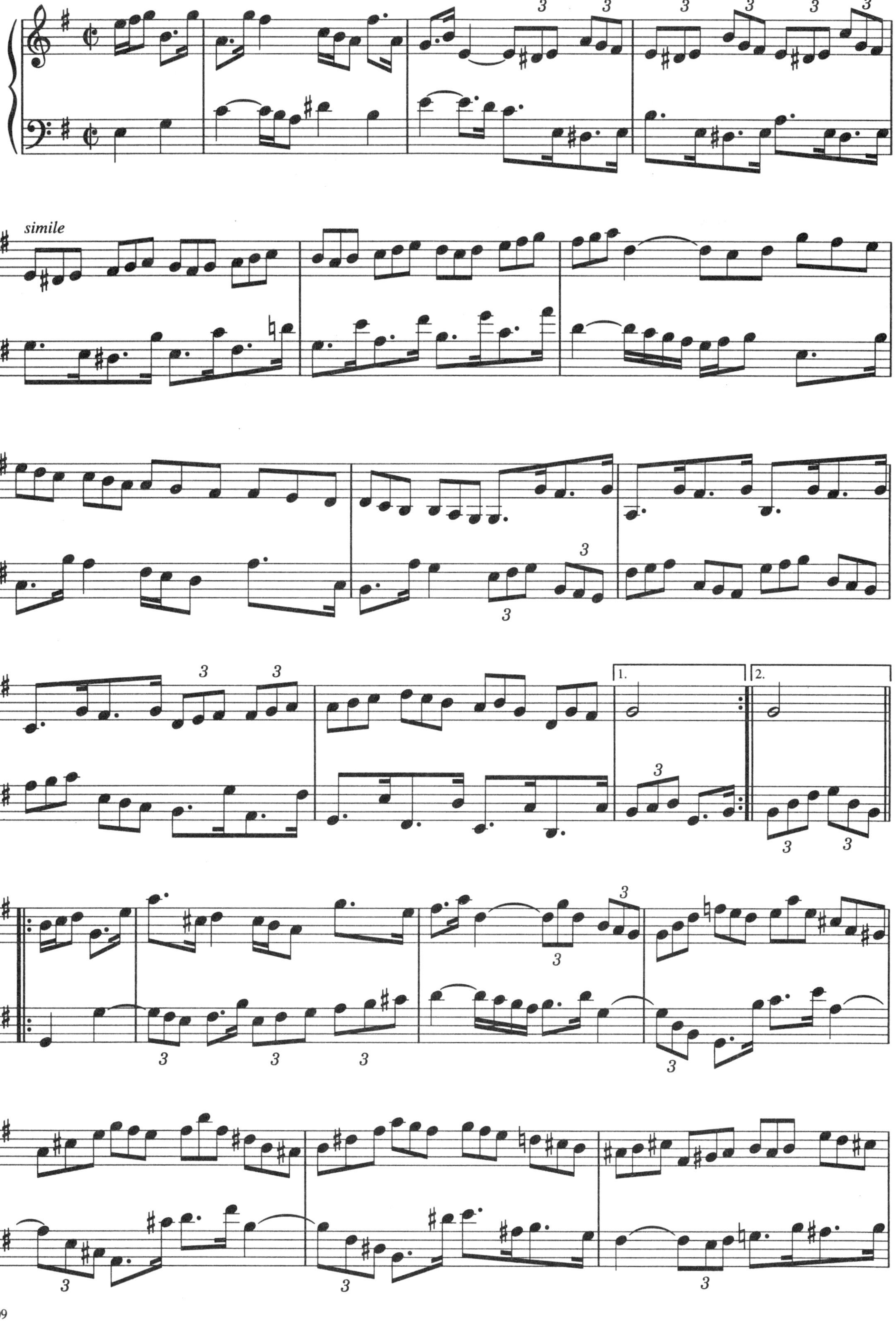

Gigue

51

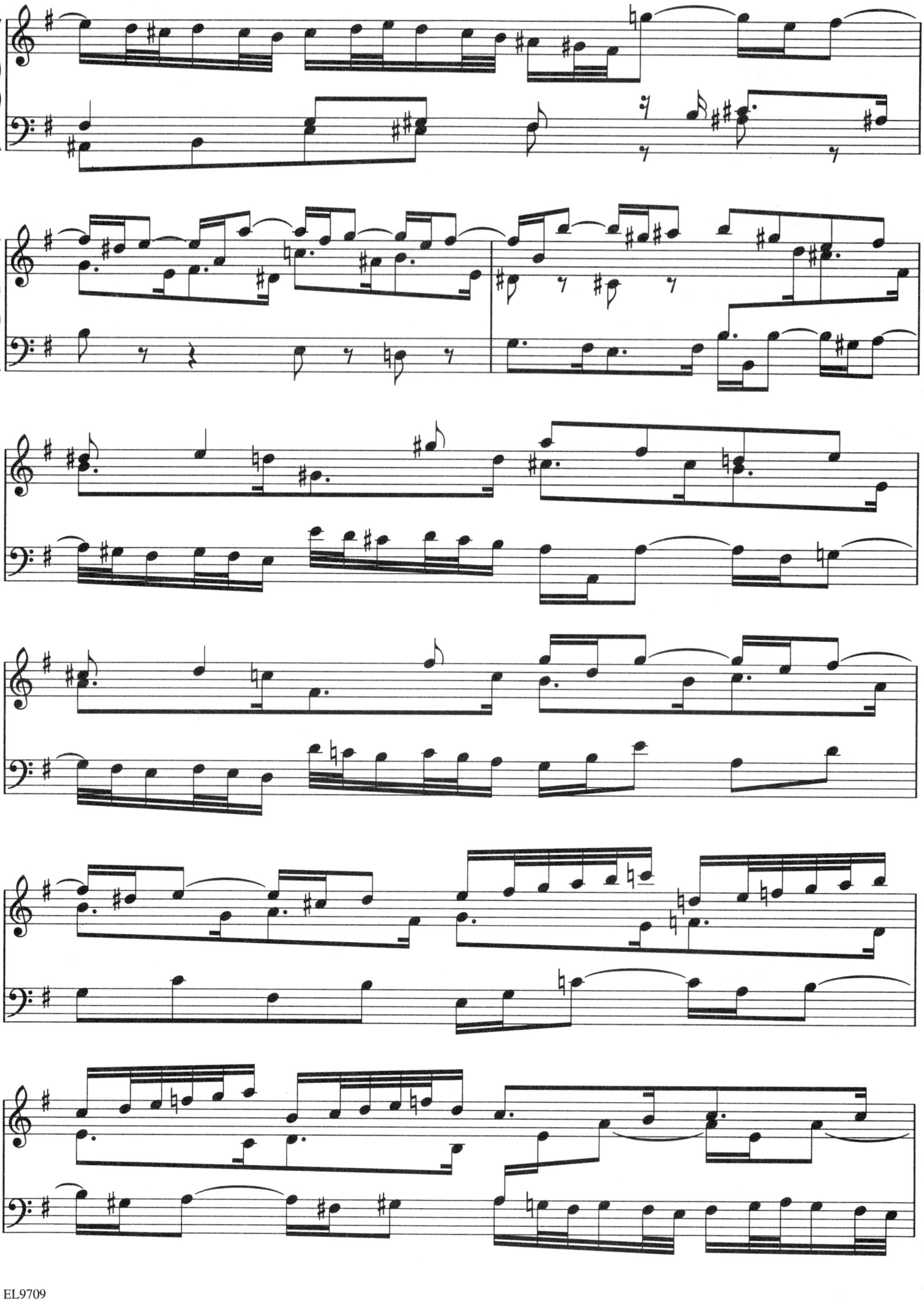

53

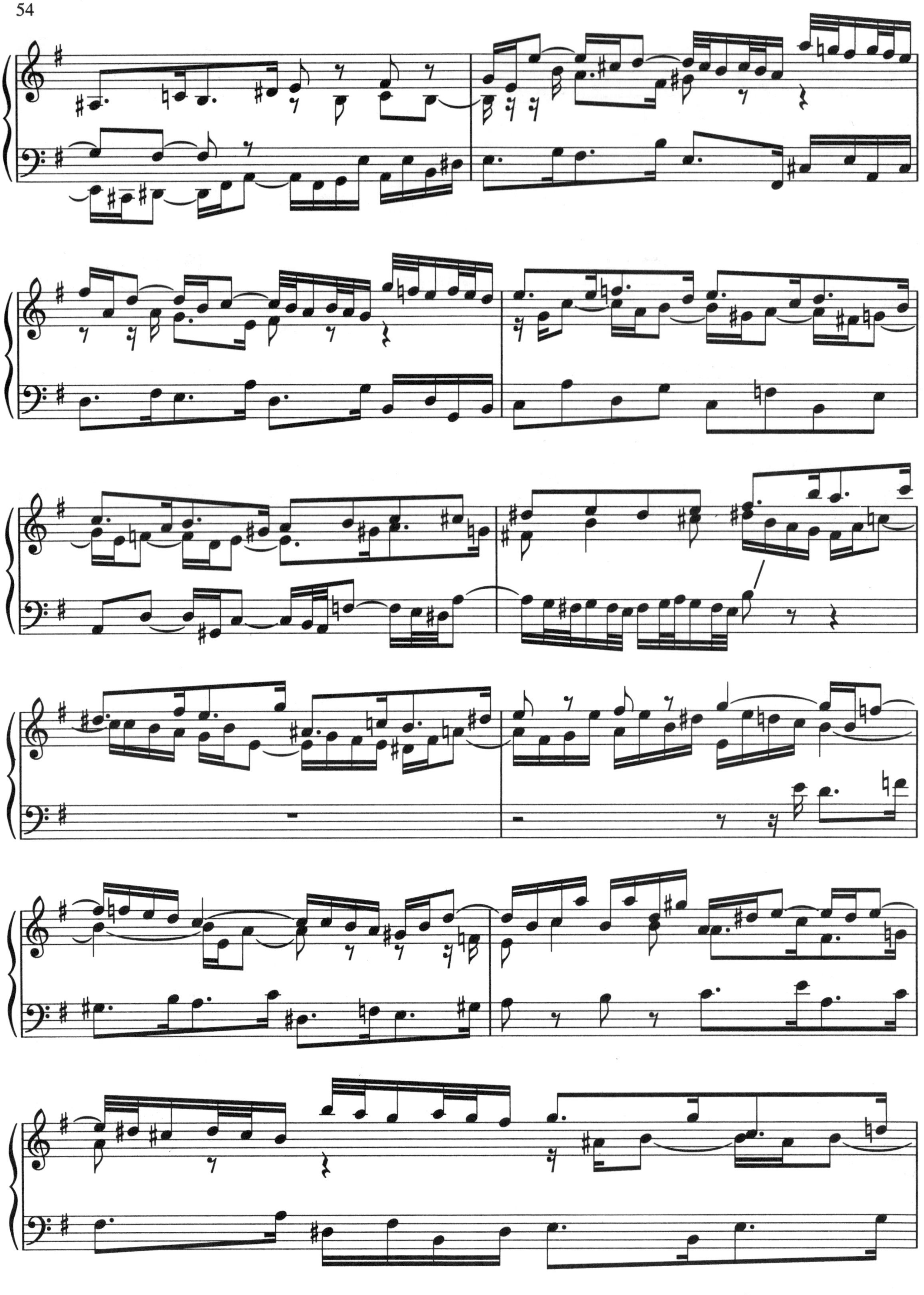

55

MENUET
in F Major

MENUET
in G Major

MENUET
in G Minor

RONDEAU
in B flat Major

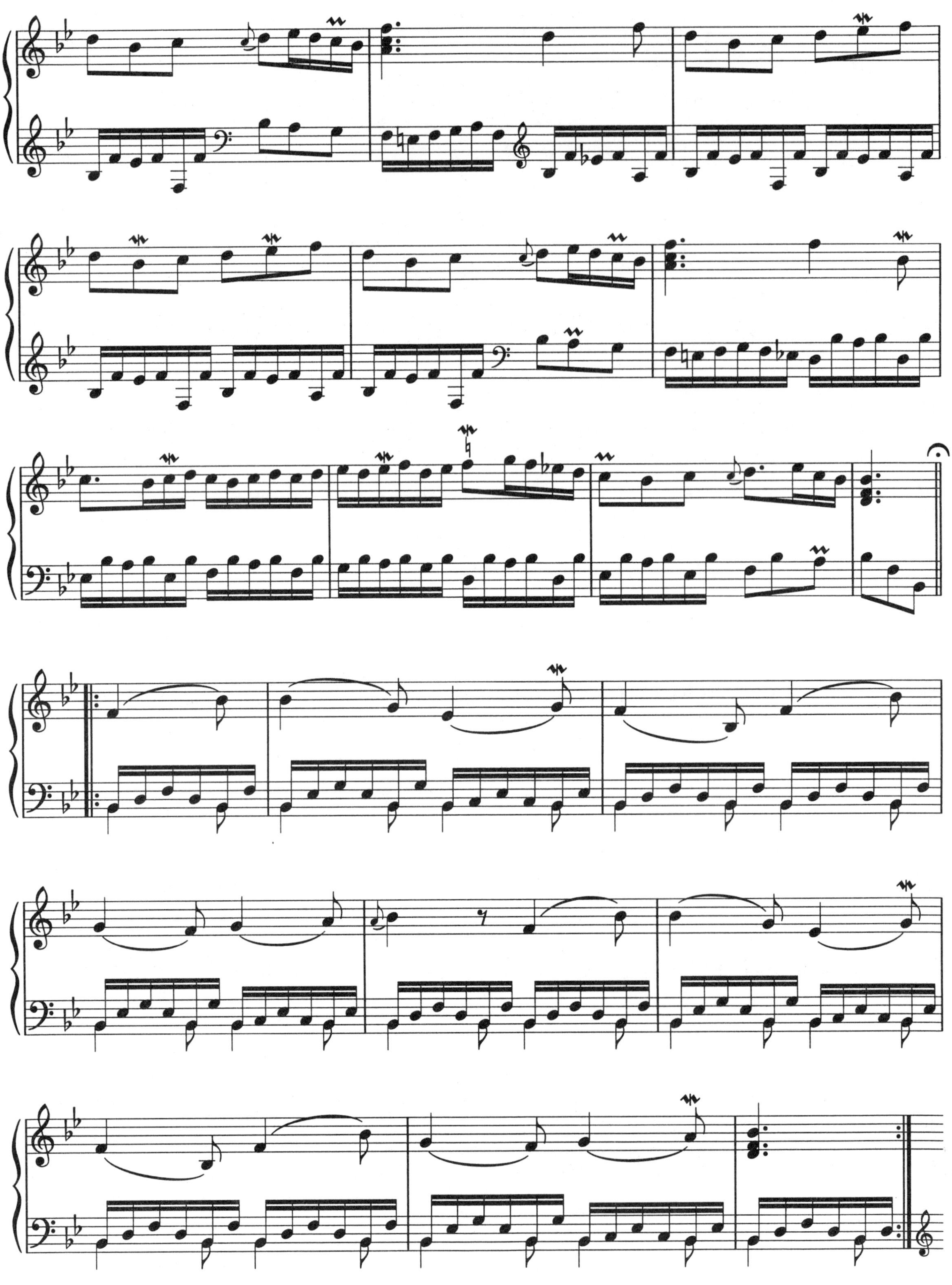

61

MENUET
in G Major

POLONAISE
in F Major

64

MENUET
in B♭ Major

POLONAISE
in G Minor

CHORALE
"Wer nur den lieben Gott lasst walten"

CHORALE
in F Major

CHORALE
"Gib dich zufrieden"

Gib dich zu - frie - den, und sei stil - le
In Ihm ruht al - ler Freu - den Fül - le,

70

in dem Got - te dei - nes Le - bens.
ohn' Ihn mühst du dich ver - ge - bens.

Er ist dein Quell und dei - ne Son - ne, scheint
täg - lich hell zu dei - ner Wen - ne. Gib
dich' zu - frie - den, zu - frie - den.

EL 9709

MENUET
in A Minor

MENUET
in C Minor

MARCH
in D Major

POLONAISE
in G Minor

75

MARCH
in G Major

POLONAISE
in G Minor

ARIA
"So oft ich meinen Tobacks-Pfiefe"

So oft ich meine Tobackspfeife mit gutem Knaster angefüllt zur Lust und Lehre bei, dass ich derselben ähnlich sei.

Zeitvertrieb ergreife, so gibt sie mir ein Trauerbild und füget diese Lehre bei, dass ich derselben ähnlich sei.

Erbauliche Gedanken eines Tabakrauchers.

So oft ich meine Tobacks-Pfeife,
Mit gutem Knaster angefüllt,
Zur Lust und Zeitwertreib ergreife,
So gibt sie mir ein Trauerbild
Und füget diese Lehre bei,
Dass ich derselben ähnlich sei.

Die Pfeife stammt von Thon und Erde,
Auch ich bin gleichfalls draus gemacht:
Auch ich muss einst zur Erde werden,
Sie fällt und bricht, eh ehr's gedacht,
Mir oftmals in der Hand entzwei,
Mein Schicksal ist auch einerlei.

Die Pfeife pflegt man nicht zu färben,
Sie bleibet weiss. Also der Schluss,
Dass ich auch dermaleins im Sterben
Dem Leibe nach erblassen muss.
Im Grabe wird der Körper auch
So schwarz, wie sie nach lungem Brauch.

Wenn man die Pfeife angezündet,
So sieht man, wie im Augenblick
Der Rauch in freier Luft verschwindet,
Nichts als die Asche bleibt zurück.
So wird des Menschen Ruhm verzehrt
Und dessen Leib in Staub verkehrt.

Wie oft geschieht's nicht bei dem Rauchen,
Dass, wenn der Stopfer nicht zur Hand,
Man pflegt t den Finger zu gebrauchen.
Dann denk ich, wenn ich mich verbrannt:
O, macht die Kohle solche Pein,
Wie heiss mag erst die Hölle sein?

Ich kann bei so gestalten Sachen
Mir bei dem Toback jederzeit
Erbauliche Gedanken machen.
Drum schmauch ich voll Zufriedenheit
Zu Land, zu Wasser und zu Haus
Mein Pfeifchen stets in Andacht aus.

This page has been left blank to avoid awkward page turns.

MENUET
in G Major

GEORG BÖHM

MUSETTE
in D Major

MARCH
in E flat Major

85

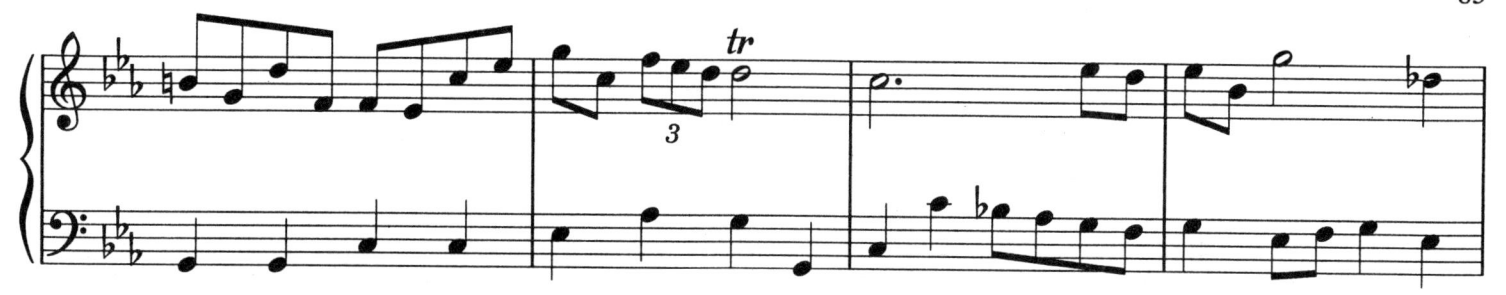

POLONAISE
in D Minor

ARIA
"Bist du bei mir"

Ach, wie vergnügt wär so mein Ende, es drückten deine schönen Hände mir die getreuen Augen zu.

Ach wie vergnügt wär so mein Ende, es drückten deine schönen Hände mir die getreuen Augen zu.

D.S. 𝄋 al Fine

SARABANDE
in G Major

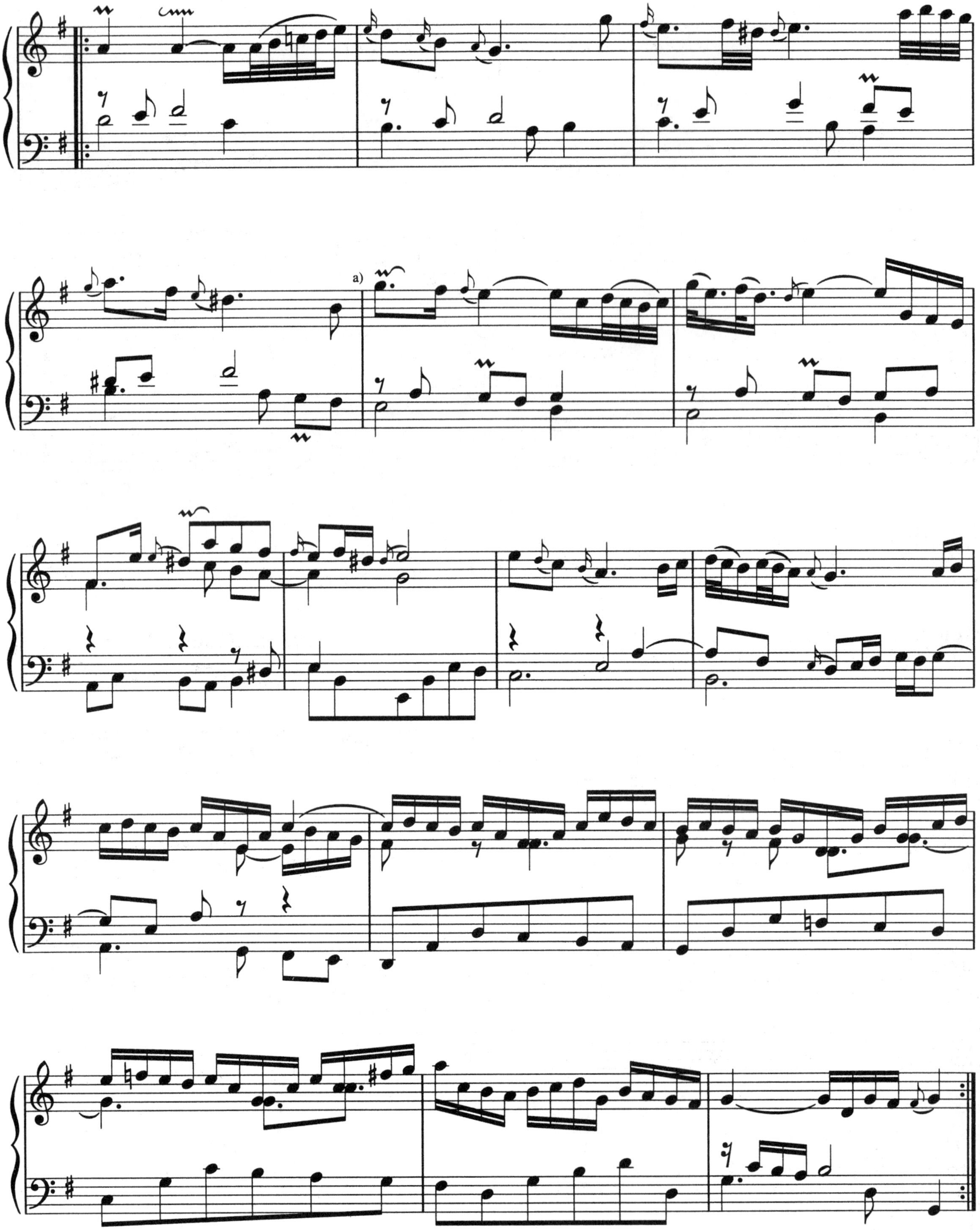

a)

b) 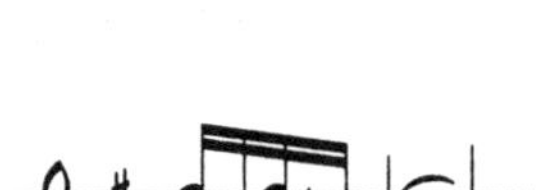

SOLO PER IL CEMBALO
in E flat Major

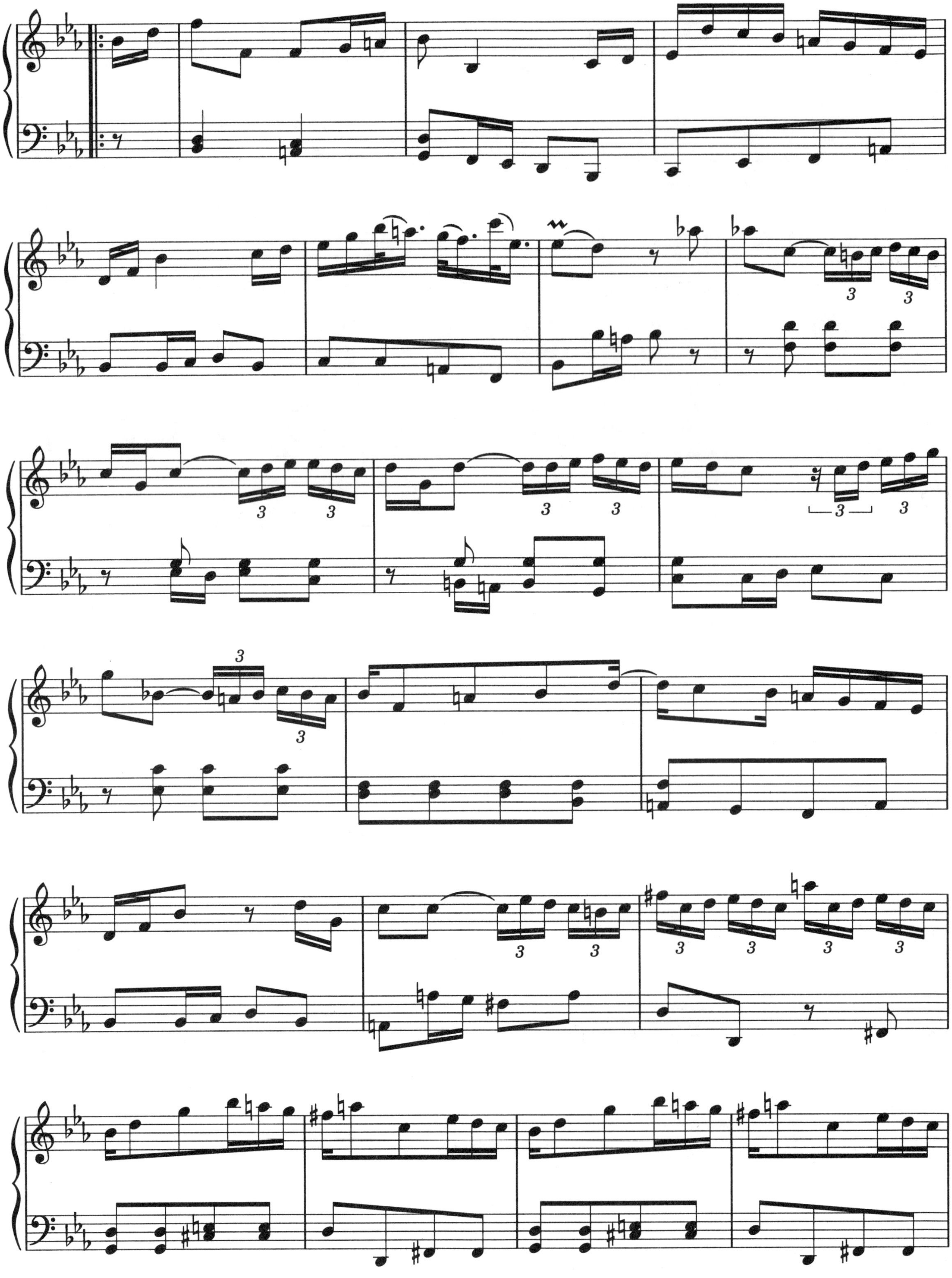
3

93

POLONAISE
in G Major

95

PRELUDE
in C Major

JOHANN SEBASTIAN BACH

97

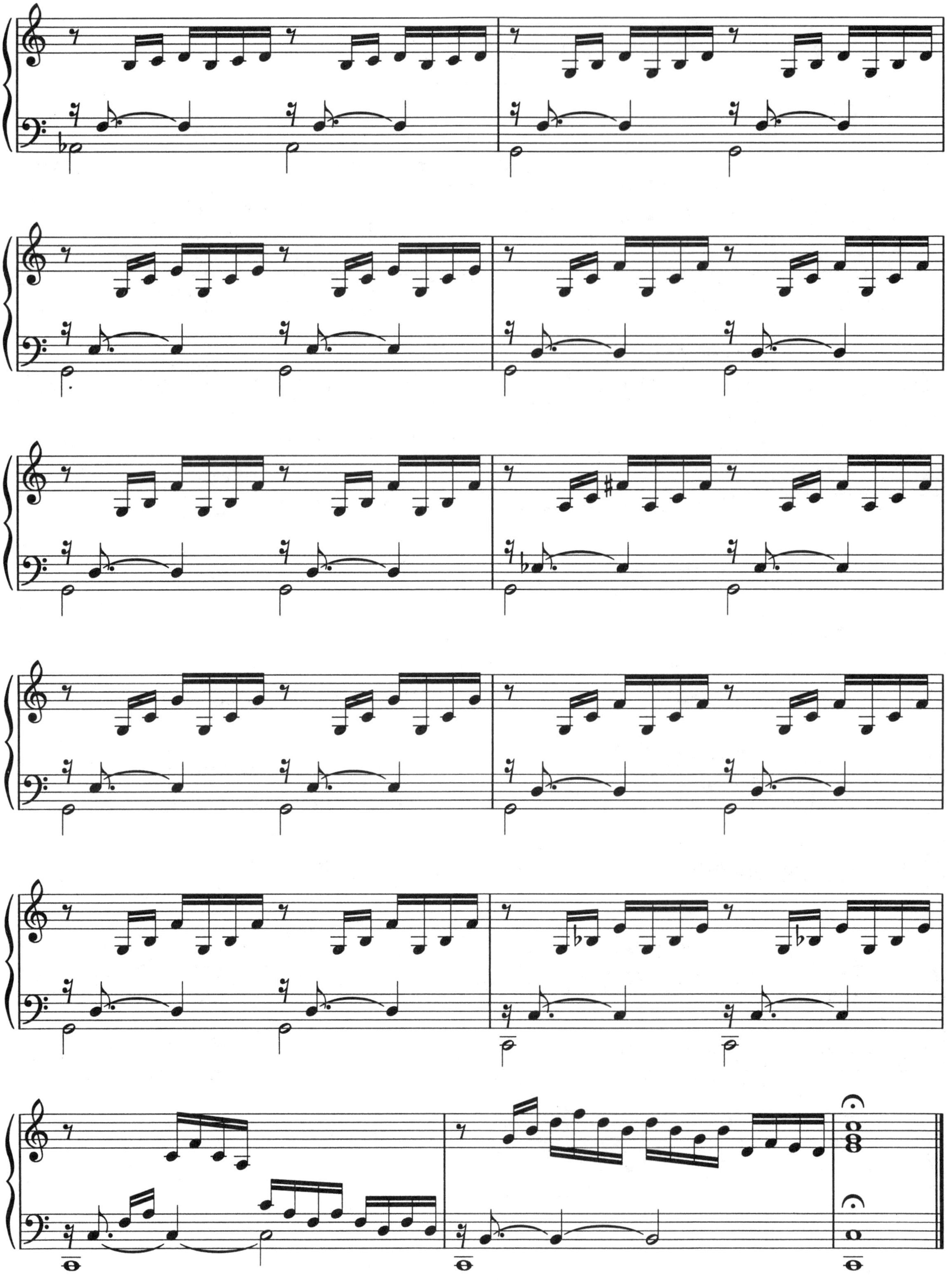

SUITE NO. 1
in D Minor

JOHANN SEBASTIAN BACH

Allemande

100

Courante

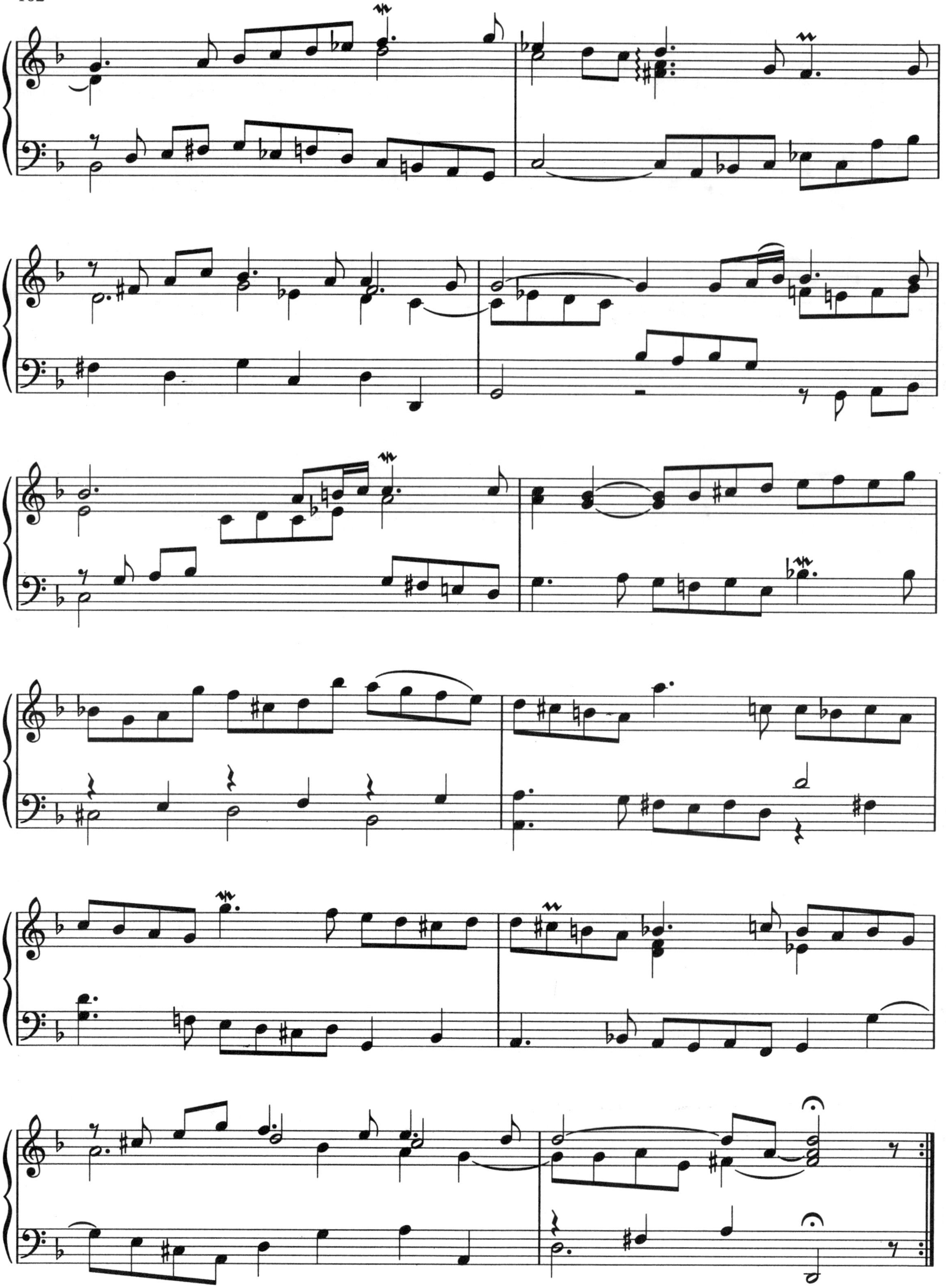

Sarabande

Menuet No. 1

Menuet No. 2

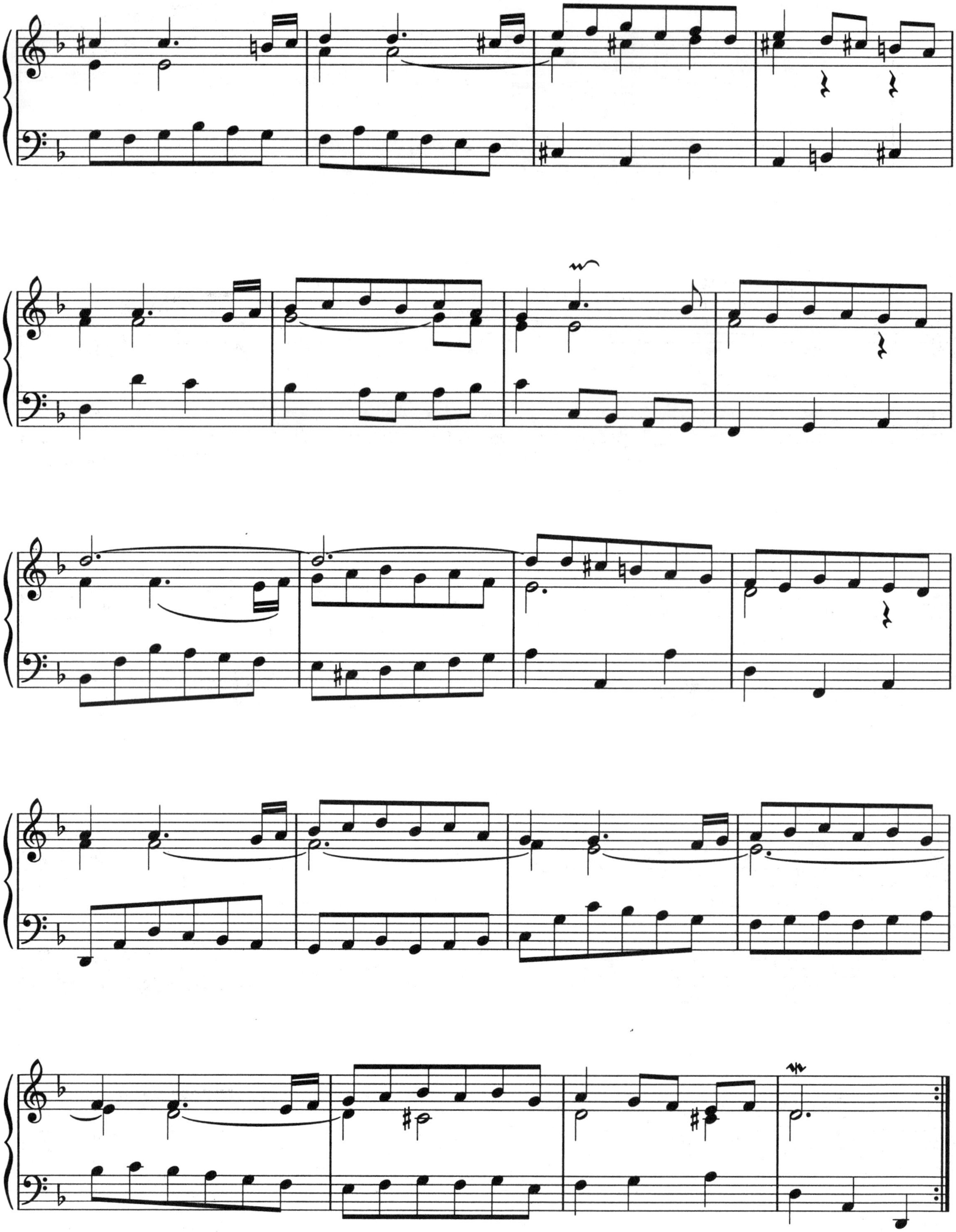

a) 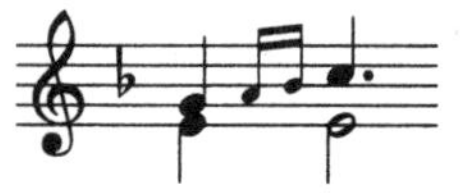

Gigue

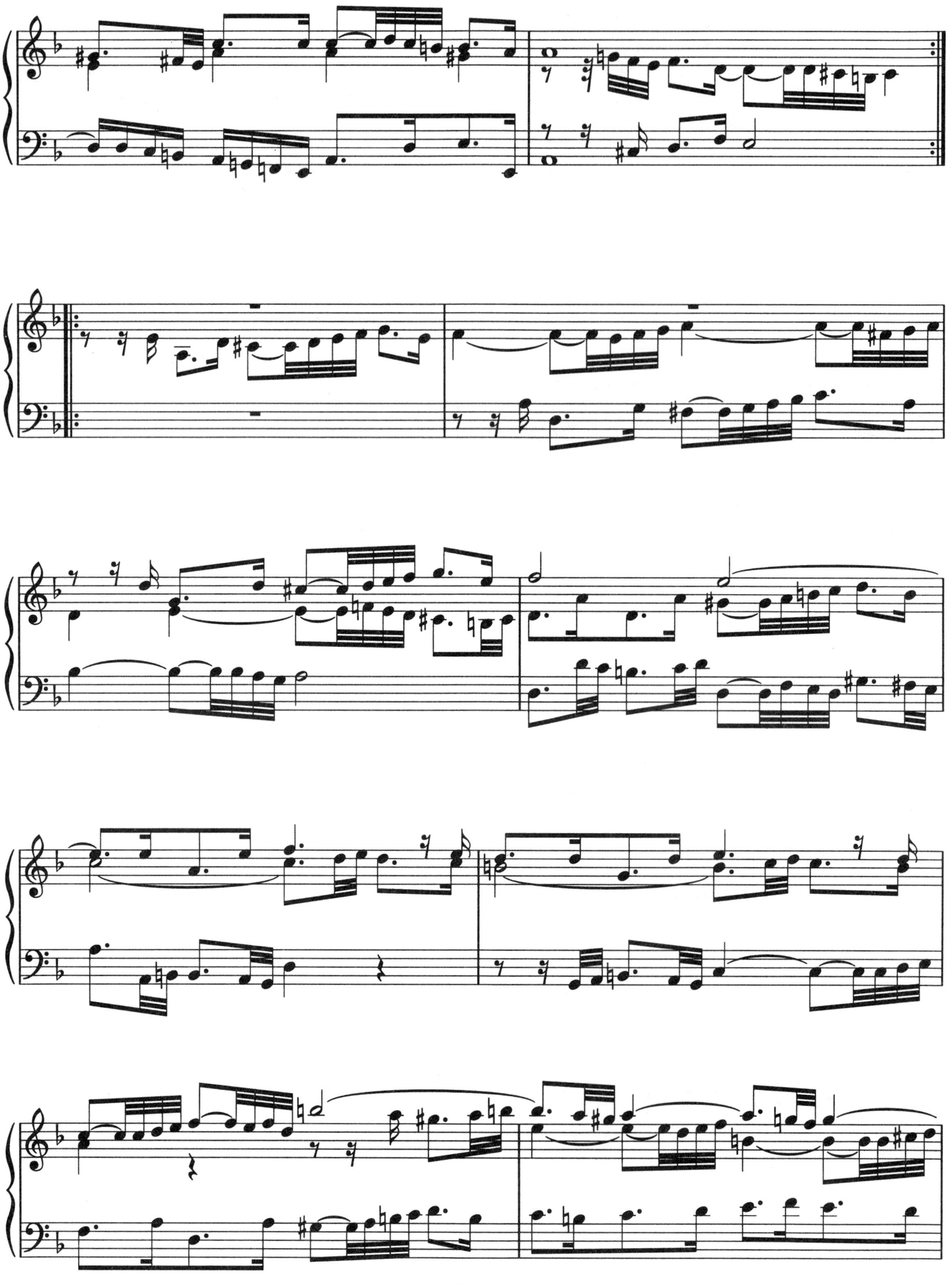

109

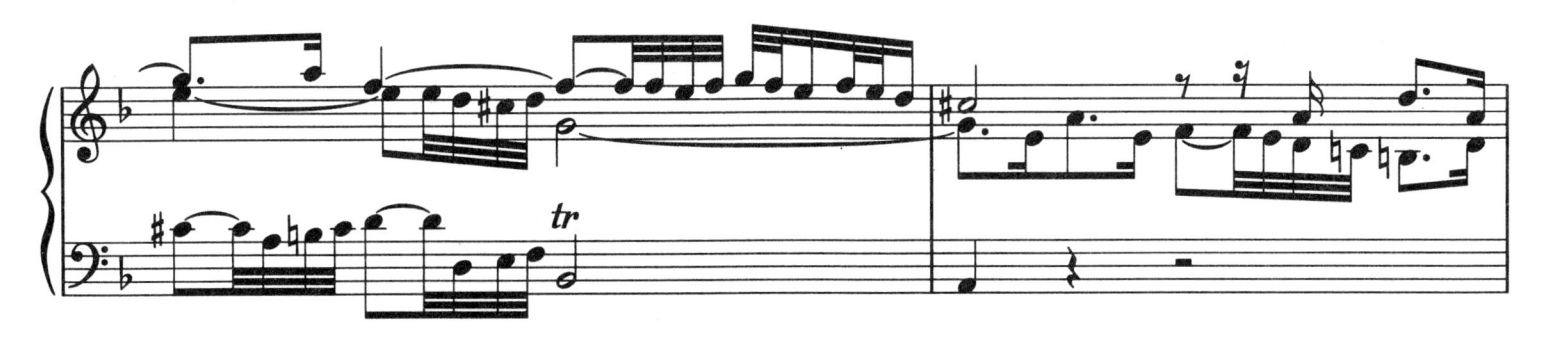

SUITE NO. 2
in C Minor

JOHANN SEBASTIAN BACH

Allemande

111

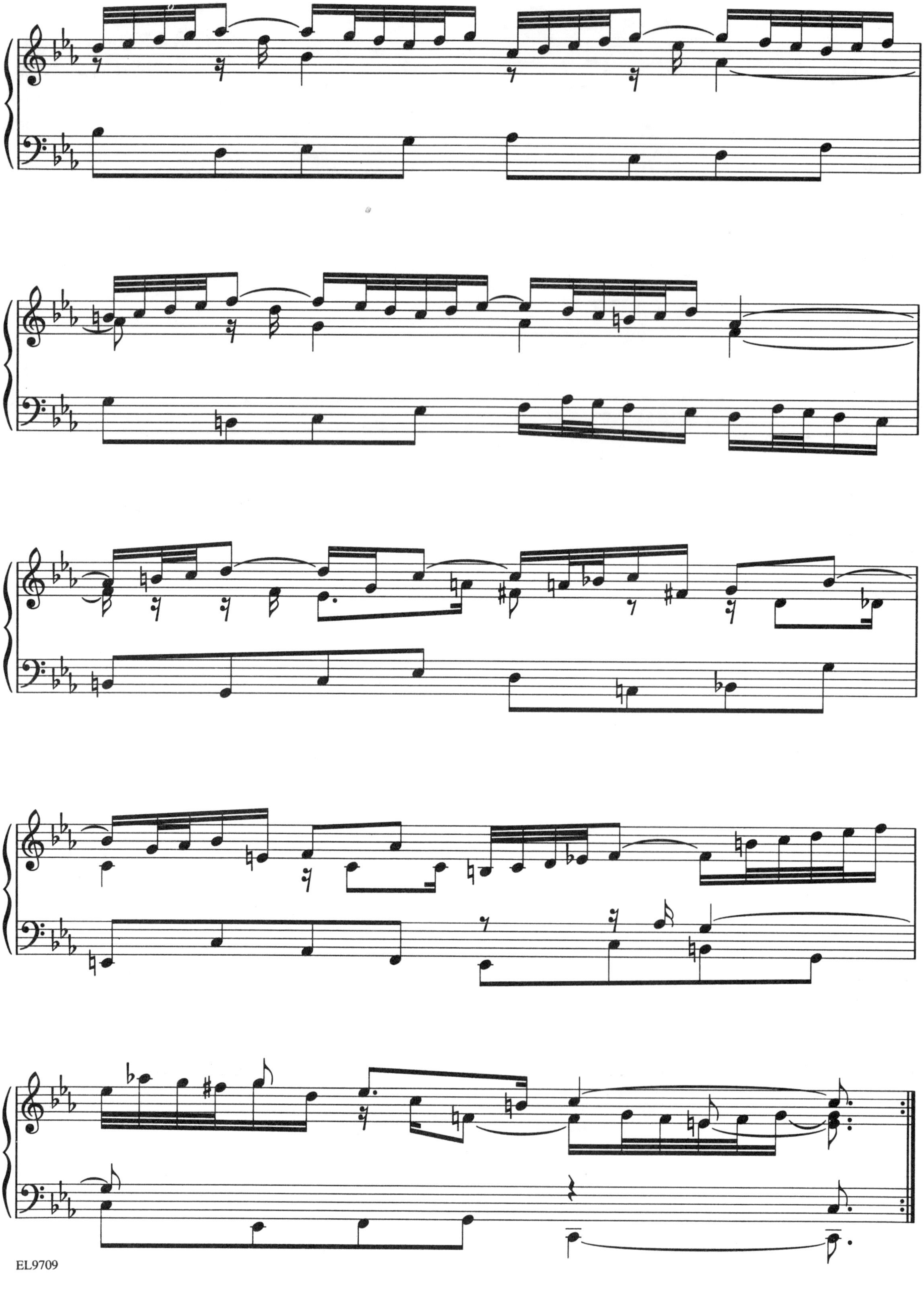

Courante

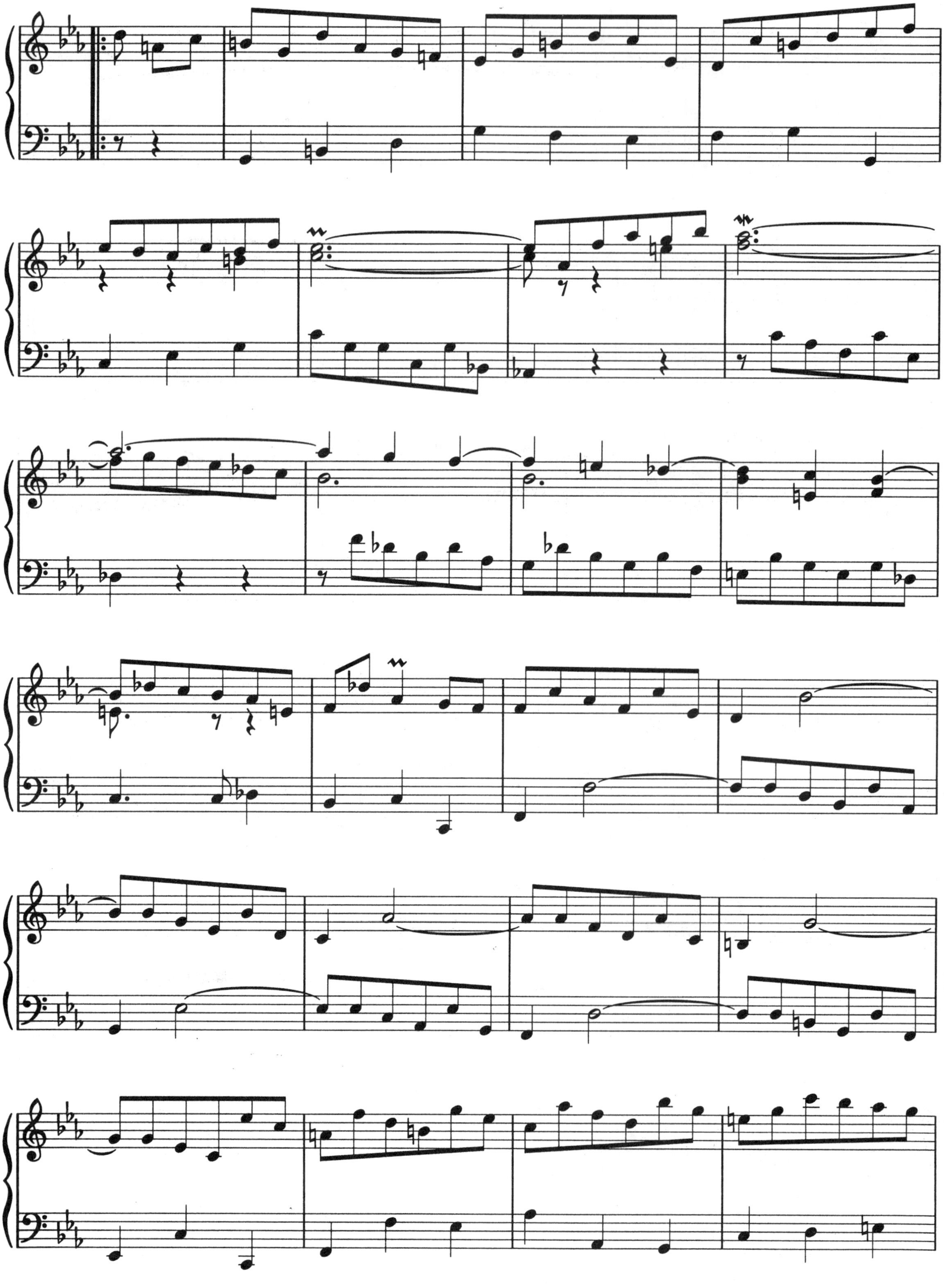

Sarabande

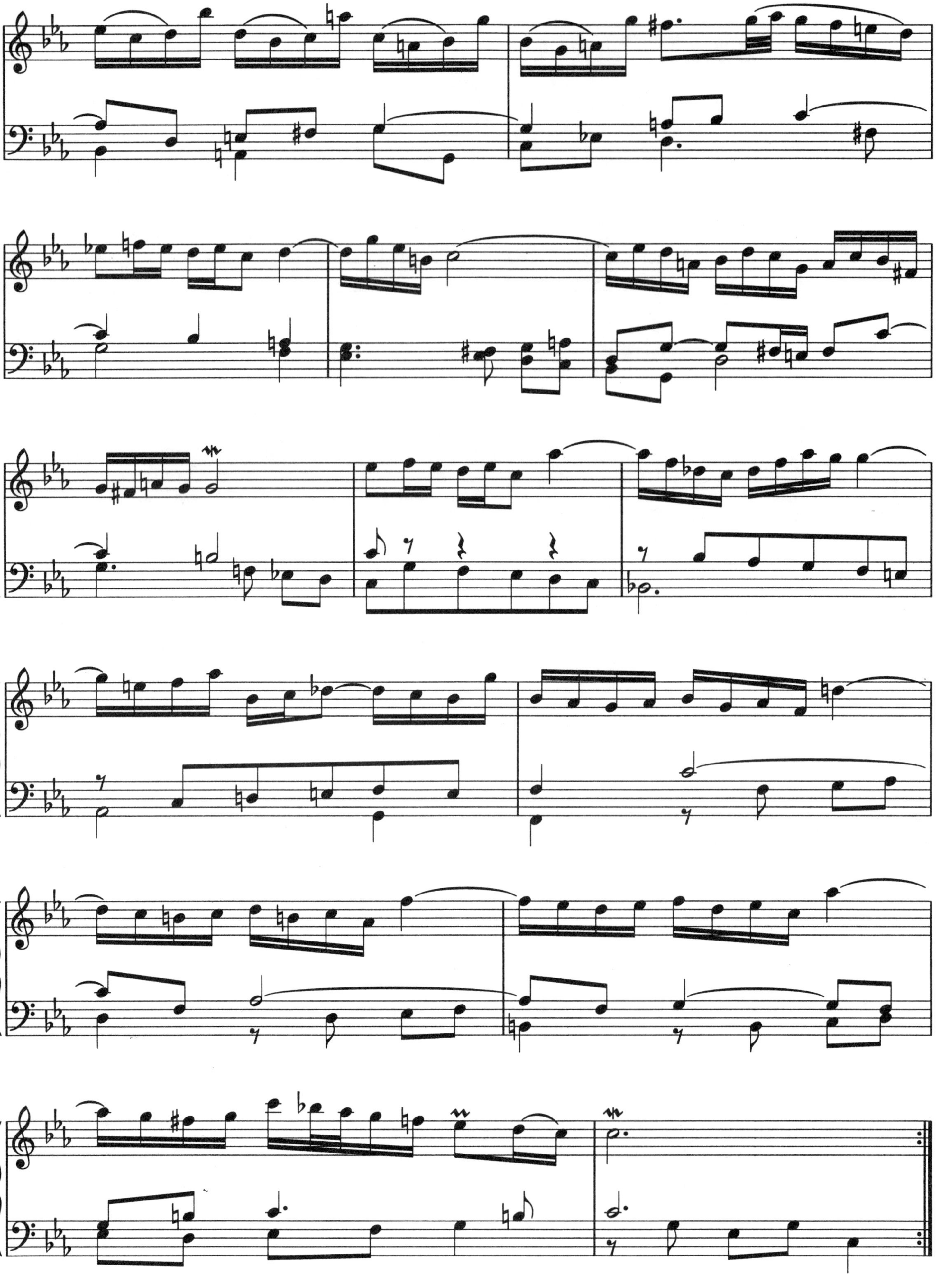

UNTITLED PIECE
in F Major

ARIA
"Warum betrübst du dich"

Wa - rum be - trübst du dich und beu - gest dich zur Er - den, mein sehr ge - plag - ter Geist, mein ab - ge - mat - ter Sinn? Wirst du dich nicht recht fest in Got - tes Wil - len grün - den, kannst du in E - wig - keit nicht wah - re Ru - he fin - den.

Du sorgst, wie will es doch noch end - lich mit dir wer - den, und fäh - rest ü - ber Welt und ü - ber Him - mel hin!

RECITATIVE AND ARIA
"Schlummert ein ihr matten Augen"

Recitative

Ich ha-be ge-nug! Mein Trost ist nur al-lein, dass Je-sus mein und ich sein ei-gen möch-te sein. Im Glau-ben halt ich ihn, da seh ich auch mit Si-me-on de Freu-de je-nes Le-bens schon. Lasst uns mit die-sem Man-ne ziehn! Ach! möch-te mich von mein-es Lei-bens Ket-ten der Herr er-ret-ten. Ach wä-re doch mein Ab-schied hier, mit

EL9709

Freu-den sagt ich, Welt zu dir: ich ha-be ge-nug.

Aria

Schlum-mert ein, ihr mat-ten Au-gen, fal-let sanft und se-lig zu, schlum-mert ein, schlum-mert ein, schlum-mert ein, ihr mat-ten Au-gen, fal-let sanft und se - lig zu! Schlum - mert ein, ihr mat - ten Au - gen, fal - let sanft und se - lig zu, fal - let sanft und se - lig zu!

Fine

Welt, ich blei - be nicht mehr hier hab' ich doch kein Teif an dir, das der See - le könn - te tau - gen, das der See - le könn - te tau - gen; Welt, ich blei - be nicht mehr hier, hab' ich doch kein Teif an dir, das -

- der See - le könn - te tau - gen.

Schlum - mert ein,

schlum -

-mert ein, schlum - mert ein
schlum - mert ein, ihr mat - ten Au - gen,
fal - let sanft und se - lig zu!
Schlum - mert ein, ihr

mat - ten Au - gen, fal - let sanft und

se - lig zu, fal - let sanft und see - lig zu!

Hier muss ich das

E - lend bau - en, a - ber dort, dort darf ich schau - en süs - sen Freu - den, stil - le Ruh,

hier muss ich das E - lend bau - en,

a - ber dort, dort werd' ich schau - en süs-

-sen Frie - den, stil - le Ruh,

Adagio

Da capo al Fine

süs - sen Frie - den, stil - le Ruh.

CHORALE
"Schaff's mit mir, Gott"

Schaff's mit mir, Gott, nach dei - nem Wil - len,
Du wirst mein Wün - schen so er - fül - len,

der sei es al - les heim - ge - stellt.
wie's dei - ner Weis - heit wohl - ge - fällt.

Du bist mein Va - ter, du wirst mich

ver - sor - gen, dar - auf hof - fe ich.

MENUET
in D Minor

ARIA DI GIOVANNINI
"Willst du dein Herz mir schenken"

Willst du dein Herz mir schen-ken, so fang' ed heim-lich an, dass un-ser bei-der Den-ken nie-mand er-ra-ten kann. Die Lie-be muss bei bei-den all-zeit ver-schwie-gen sein, drum schliess die gröss-ten Freu-den in dei-nem Her-zen ein.

Be-hut-sam sei und schwei-ge und trau-e kei-ner Wand, lieb' in-ner-lich und zei-ge dich aus-sen un-be-kannt. Kein Arg-wohn musst du ge-ben, Ver-stel-lung nö-tig ist, ge-nug, dass du, mein Le-ben, der Treu' ver-si-chert bist.

Verse 3: Begehre keine Blicke von meiner Liebe nich't,
Der Neid hat viele Stüke auf unser Tun gericht't.
Du musst die Brust verschliessen, halt' deine Neigung ein,
Die Lust, die wir geniessen, muss ein Geheimnis sein.

Verse 4: Zu frei sein, sich ergehen, hat oft Gefahr gebracht,
Man muss sich wohl verstehen, weil ein falsch Auge wacht
Du musst den Spruch bedenken, den ich zuvor getan:
Willst du deun Herz mir schenken, so fang es heimlich an.

This page has been left blank to avoid awkward page turns.

CHORALE
"Dir, dir Jehovah, will ich singen"
(four voices)

Dir, dir, Jehovah, will ich singen,
Dir will ich meine Lieder bringen:
denn wo ist so ein solcher Gott, wie du?
ach! gib mir deines Geistes Kraft darzu,

dass ich es tu' im Namen Jesu Christ, so
dass ich es tu' im Namen Jesu Christ, so
dass ich es tu' im Namen Jesu Christ, so
dass ich es tu' im Namen Jesu Christ, so

wie es dir durch ihn gefällig ist.
wie es dir durch ihn gefällig ist.
wie es dir durch ihn gefällig ist.
wie es dir durch ihn gefällig ist.

CHORALE
"Dir, dir Jehovah, will ich singen"

Dir, dir, Jehovah, will ich singen,
Dir will ich meine Lieder bringen:
Zeuch mich, o Vater, zu' dem Sohne,
Dein Geist in meinem Herzen wohne,

denn wo ist so ein solcher Gott, wie du?
ach! gib mir deines Geistes Kraft darzu,
damit dein Sohn mich' wieder zeih zu dir.
und meine Sinnen und Verstand regier',

dass ich es tu' im Namen Jesu Christ, so
dass ich den Frieden Gottes schmeck' und fühl, und

Verse 3: Verleih mir, Höchster, solche Güte, so wird gewiss mein Singen recht getan;
So klingt es schön in meinem Liede, und ich bet' dich in Geist und Wahrheit an;
so hebt dein Geist mein Herz zu dir empor, dass ich dir Psalmen sing im höhern Chor.

Verse 4: Denn der kann mich bei dir vertreten mit Seufzern, die ganz unaussprechlich sind,
der lehret mich recht, gläubig beten, gibt Zeugnis meinem Geist, dass ich dein Kind.
und ein Miterbe Jesu Christi sei, daher ich Abba, lieber Vater! schrei.

Verse 5: Wenn dies aus meinem Herzen schallet durch deines heilgen Geistes Kraft und Trieb,
so bricht dein Vaterherz und wallet ganz brünstig gegen mich vor heisser lieb'.
dass mir's die Bitte nicht versagen kann, die ich nach deinem Willen hab getan.

Verse 6: Was mich dein Geist selbst bitten lehret, das ist nach deinem Willen eingericht't.
und wird gewiss von dir erhöret, weil es in Namen deines Sohns geschlicht,
durch welchen ich dein Kind und Erbe bin, und nehme von dir Gnad' um Gnade hin.

Verse 7: Wohl mir, dass ich dies Zeugnis habe, so bin ich voller Trost und Freudigkeit;
und weiss, dass alle gute Gabe, die ich verlange, erlange jederzeit,
die gibst du und tust überschwenglich mehr, als ich ver stehe, bitte und begehr.

Verse 8: Wohl mir, ich bitt' in Jesu Namen, der mich zu deiner Rechten selbst vertritt,
in ihm ist alles Ja und Amen, was ich von dir im Geist and Glauben bitt'.
Wohl mir, Lob dir itzt und un Ewigkeit dass du mir schenkest solche Seligkeit.

ARIA
"Wie wohl ist mir, O Freund der Seelen"

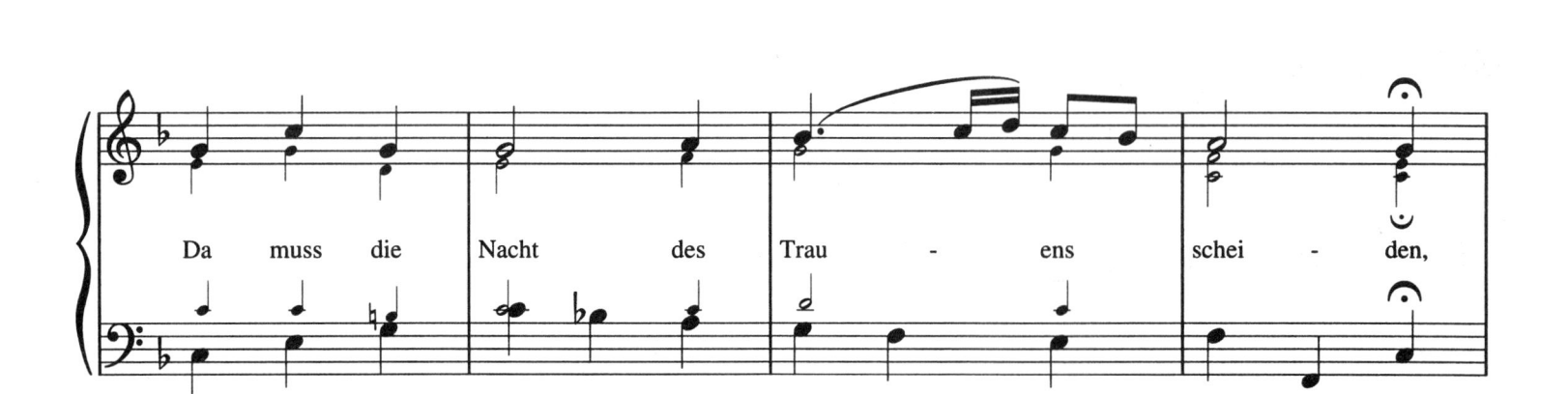

Wie wohl ist mir, o Freund der See - len,
Ich stei - ge aus der Schwer - muts höh - len
wenn ich in dei - ner Lie - be ruh',
und ei - le dei - nen Ar - men zu.
Da muss die Nacht des Trau - ens schei - den,
wenn mit so an - ge - neh - mem Freu - den

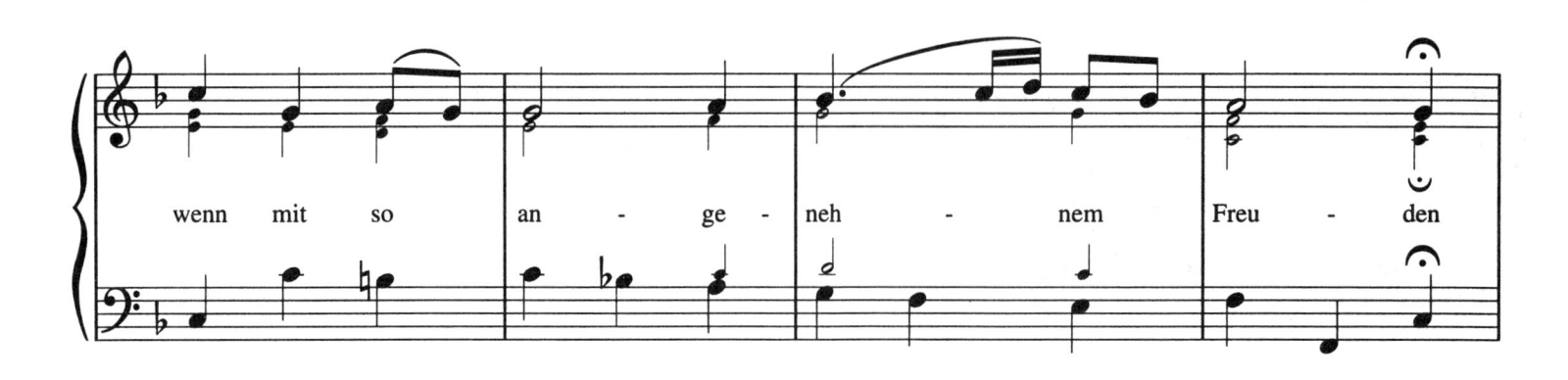

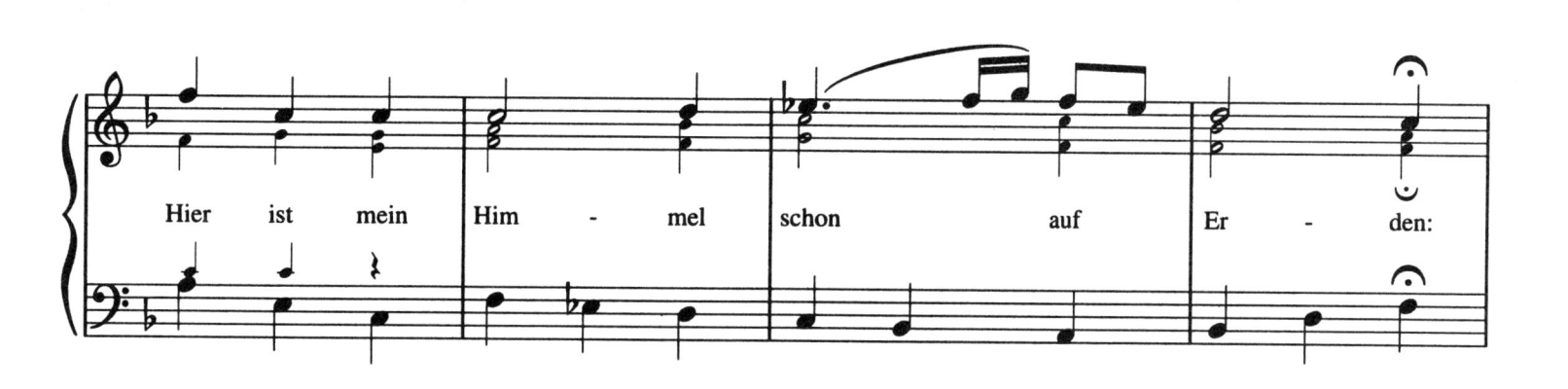

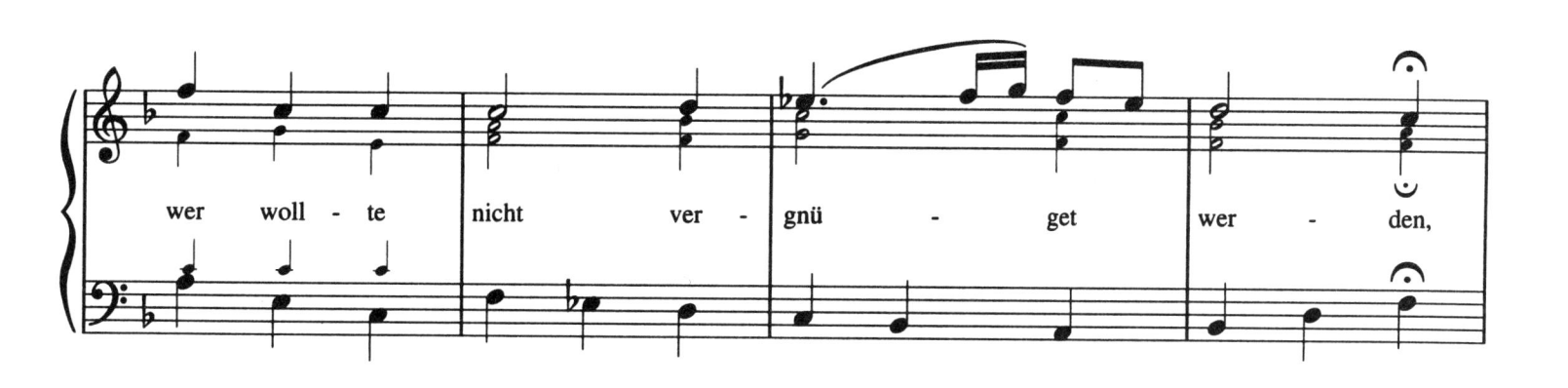

die Lie - be strahlt aus mei - ner Brust.

Hier ist mein Him - mel schon auf Er - den:

wer woll - te nicht ver - gnü - get wer - den,

der in dir fin - det Ruh' und Lust.

ARIA
"Gedenke doch, mein Geist, zurücke"

Gedenke doch, mein Geist, zurükke ans Grab und an den Glokkenschlag, da man mich wird zur Ruh' be-glei-ten, auf dass ich klüg-lich ster-ben mag. Schreib die-ses Wort in Herz und Brust ge-den-ke, dass du ster-ben musst.

CHORALE
"O Ewigkeit, du Donnerwort"